MILK
BAR:
KIDS
ONLY

CHRISTINA TOSI

MILK BAR: KIDS ONLY

CLARKSON POTTER /

PUBLISHERS

NEW YORK

Published in the United States by Clarkson Potter/
Publishers, an imprint of Random House, a division of
Penguin Random House LLC, New York.
clarksonpotter.com

CLARKSON POTTER is a trademark and POTTER
with colophon is a registered trademark of
Penguin Random House LLC.

Library of Congress Cataloging-in-Publication Data
is available upon request.

ISBN 978-0-593-23192-0
Ebook ISBN 978-0-593-23193-7

Printed in the United States of America

10 9 8 7 6 5 4 3 2 1

First Edition

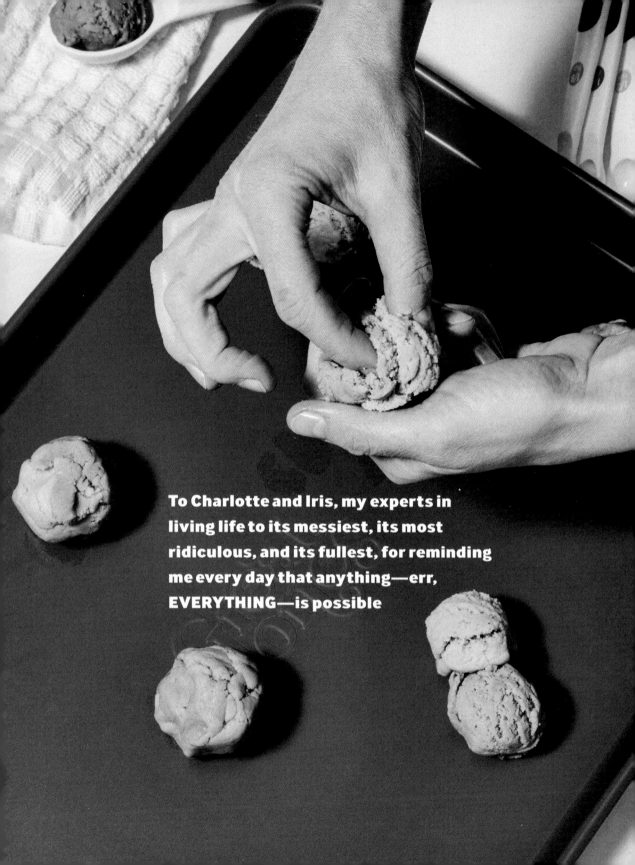

To Charlotte and Iris, my experts in living life to its messiest, its most ridiculous, and its fullest, for reminding me every day that anything—err, EVERYTHING—is possible

CONTENTS

RECIPES BY TYPE
8

INTRODUCTION
11

RULES OF THE KITCHEN
14

PANTRY 411
17

TOOLS OF THE TRADE
20

MEASURING 101: WETS, DRIES, AND DONENESS
22

HELP HOTLINE!
24

THE RECIPES
26

SHOUT-OUTS
233

INDEX
235

RECIPES BY TYPE

This book is organized like a calendar: It starts with recipes we enjoy in January and runs through December. You know I am a fan of shaking things up, so if you want to make Jack-o'-Lantern Muffins in May instead of October, you have a big thumbs-up from me. This checklist will help you explore all year round.

BARS

- ❑ Triple Layer Cheesecake Bars 30
- ❑ White Chocolate Blondies 53
- ❑ Dreamsicle Blondies 82
- ❑ Easy as Pie Bars 85
- ❑ Gazillionaire's Bars 97
- ❑ DIY Ice Cream Sandwiches 146

CEREAL TREATS + NO BAKES

- ❑ Coco Cabana Cereal Squares 33
- ❑ Rocky Road Cereal Squares 54
- ❑ Citrus Surprise Cereal Squares 65
- ❑ Rise and Shine Cereal Squares 71
- ❑ Cherry Pie Cereal Squares 151
- ❑ Compost Cereal Squares 152
- ❑ PB&J Cereal Squares 167
- ❑ Apple-a-Day Cereal Squares 188
- ❑ B-Day Cereal Squares 227

CUPCAKES + A CAKE

- ❑ Berry Loco Cupcakes 41
- ❑ Chocolate Coconut Cupcakes 93
- ❑ Strawberries and Cream Cupcakes 109
- ❑ Black and White Cupcakes 168
- ❑ Pumpkin Patch Cupcakes 181
- ❑ Grasshopper Cupcakes 206
- ❑ Candy Cane Lane Sheet Cake 217

CUT-OUT + SANDWICH COOKIES

- ❑ Chocolate Cut-Out Cookies 26
- ❑ Building Blocks Cookie Sandwiches 35
- ❑ Nut-n-Jammie Cookie Sammies 102
- ❑ Cut-Out Cookies 141
- ❑ Fluffermutter Cookie Sandwiches 155
- ❑ Nutty Sandies 172
- ❑ Gingerbread Cut-Out Cookies 213

DROP COOKIES

- ❑ Choco Crunch Cookies 48
- ❑ Earth Day Cookies 69
- ❑ Mint Cookies and Cream Cookie Pie 89
- ❑ Granola Cookies 101
- ❑ Best Chocolate Chip Cookies Ever (To Me, Anyway) 135
- ❑ Lemonade Zing Cookies 191
- ❑ Cinnamon Butterscotch Cookies 192
- ❑ Birthday Cookies 224
- ❑ Chocolate Birthday Cookies 225

MUFFINS

- ❑ French Toast Muffins 29
- ❑ Monkey in the Middle Muffins 74
- ❑ Veggie Frittata Bites 81
- ❑ Tropical Mermaid Muffins 107
- ❑ Chocolate Muffins 112
- ❑ Berries and Cream Muffins 123
- ❑ Bacon-Cheddar Cornbake Muffins 129
- ❑ Jack-o'-Lantern Muffins 184
- ❑ Power Muffins 195

PANCAKES + WAFFLES

- ☐ Compost Pancakes 38
- ☐ German Chocolate Cake Waffles 47
- ☐ Really Good Flapjacks 62
- ☐ Blueberry-Lemon Pancakes 78
- ☐ Leftover Waffle 86
- ☐ Corn Dog Waffles 125
- ☐ Apple Pie Waffles 162
- ☐ Mac 'n' Cheese Pancakes 196
- ☐ S'mores Pancake Cake 199
- ☐ Birthday Pancakes 231

QUICK LOAVES

- ☐ Banana Crunch Bread 57
- ☐ Bird Bread 66
- ☐ Raspberry-Lemon Ricotta Tea Cake 98
- ☐ Cornbread 118
- ☐ Pizza Bread 176
- ☐ Cinnamon-Bun Quick Bread 211

SHORTCAKES + BISCUITS

- ☐ Cheddar Chive Biscuits 73
- ☐ Strawberry Shortcakes 130
- ☐ Cinnamon Sugar and Peach Shortcakes 137
- ☐ Give a Dog a Biscuit 174
- ☐ Biscuit Eggs in a Frame 201
- ☐ Ham and Jam Biscuits 204
- ☐ B-Day Shortcake Sundaes 228

SMOOTHIES, SHAKES + A QUAKE

- ☐ Snow Ice Cream 44
- ☐ Pot o' Gold Shakes 61
- ☐ Chunky Monkey Smoothies 75
- ☐ Watermelon Lime Smoothies 104
- ☐ Donut Shakes 114
- ☐ Snap Crackle Pop Shakes 117
- ☐ Peaches and Cream Smoothies 121
- ☐ All-the-Fruit Smoothies 121
- ☐ Purple Cow Floats 126
- ☐ Anything Goes Shakes 158
- ☐ Flower Power Smoothies 161
- ☐ Popcorn Shakes 177
- ☐ Trick-or-Treat Quakes 187
- ☐ Cookies and (Ice) Cream Shakes 220

HELLO AND WELCOME TO

MILK BAR: KIDS ONLY!

My name is Christina, and I own Milk Bar, a bakery where I serve up my spin on cookies, cakes, pies, and ice cream—but my love of all things dessert started way, way before I was old enough to pay rent.

Both my parents worked, and most days after school, I simply couldn't wait for them to get home to help me turn on the oven. I'd figure out ways to concoct cookie dough or cereal treats, cake batters and icings. My creations were great in my eyes, but judging by the looks on my sister Angela's face, I was mad crazy to think they were serve-able. Edible, even. But that didn't matter much to me. I loved playing with ingredients, learning time and time again how to dig deep into the pantry and create something new, something epic, something that was all mine.

I always thought my mom's advice of "Just be yourself" was lip service—the kind of thing parents tell you but that doesn't really solve any of your problems. Little did I know that it would one day be the phrase I tell myself when I get dressed in the morning, when I'm choosing whether or not candy bars between bread is an acceptable lunch sandwich to pack, when I walk into the Milk Bar kitchen or the *MasterChef Junior* kitchen or a big, adult boardroom meeting. It's certainly what I tell myself when I'm dreaming up my next cake flavor combo (pretzel–potato chip–chocolate-butterscotch-graham?!) or deciding whether or not corn dog waffles are a good idea (they're out of this world, in case you were wondering).

The cool part about being a kid—that's you!—is that you're naturally much closer to the spirit of "Just be yourself." I'm sure there are things that you worry about in life, but if you're like lots of kids, you don't know how to be anything *but* yourself. I mean, you're probably still learning and tinkering with the very idea of what "yourself" is! So you create, come up with ideas, and express them freely, willing to try anything and everything that comes to mind. Your imagination knows no limit. This is the kind of world I believe in. And when it comes to baking, I believe there is no better way to be.

As a kind-of adult, I think we need to give kids like you more room to spread your wings and fly. You are so unbelievably capable and curious. You see, you listen, you understand—and when you don't, you're hungry to learn. You are old enough to know your likes and dislikes but young enough to be unapologetically fearless in your pursuit of a wacky cheddar-chive biscuit ham sandwich or gingerbread peace-sign cookies with a cranberry glaze. You have boundless passion and fresh ideas, and that's what this world needs most: the magic you have within—magic you measure and mix, magic you deliver to the table and into the world beyond.

I wanted to write this cookbook because it's the cookbook I didn't have when I was growing up. It's a cookbook that teaches the basics, then encourages you to see the brilliance that a little personality can bring to the mix. It's a cookbook I hope you will make your weekend plans and parties around. It's a book that gives you permission to make a mess, to let your truest self run wild and share that part of you with your family, neighbors, and friends. There is also a section about cleaning up, I promise.

XO, TOSI

P.S. I hope it's also a book that you take with you as you grow up, a reminder that you can be anything in life now and forever, as long as it's yourself.

HERE ARE A FEW QUICK TIPS ON HOW TO USE THIS BOOK:

· **This book is organized by the time of year.** It starts in the winter and runs through the rest of the seasons. Think of it like a baking calendar. You can open up to a season and find a recipe to help you celebrate a holiday or an in-season ingredient. But don't let that box you in; if you want to bake gingerbread cookies in July, do YOU. If you are feeling super uninspired, just try flipping to a random page! Oh, and since the very best holiday of all—BIRTHDAYS!—happens all year-round, you'll find our favorite b'day recipes grouped together at the end.

· **I'm sharing with you my all-time favorite basic recipes,** from a really, really good cut-out cookie to an out-of-this-world strawberry frosting—and I've also included some suggestions on how to pair them together. Once you master the basics, the next step is to mix and match, like a baker-meets–mad scientist.

· **I have complete faith that you are going to absolutely crush these recipes.** But every now and again, where you might need just a little help from me, I include some additional technique instructions and photos to help guide you.

· **Read the "Rules of the Kitchen" (page 14)** and the ingredients and equipment sections (see pages 17–21) before you dive in. They'll help give you lay of the land.

RULES OF THE KITCHEN

1. THERE ARE NO RULES.
Truth time: Most of the time, I learn the rules for doing something only so I can find out how I can break them. In life we are so often told that things need to be a certain way, that success looks and sounds like x, y, and z. To that I say, "Don't box me in, world!" If you want to have cookies for breakfast and birthday cake on a random Wednesday, you CAN. If you want to be a CEO who wears sneakers and tie-dyed tees to work, go for it. We like to think of ourselves as joy detectives, hunting down happiness wherever we can find it—and that might just mean popping up a tent in my living room because toaster-oven s'mores just taste better in a sleeping bag. Go ahead and break "the rules." I won't tell if you won't. That said, there are some things I tell everyone to keep in mind when they're in the kitchen.

2. SET YOURSELF UP FOR SUCCESS.
There is no bigger bummer than getting halfway through a recipe and realizing you don't have a key ingredient. Before you start mixing and whisking, take a beat to read through the whole recipe, collect all your ingredients and tools, and formulate a little game plan. Reading through the recipe

fully before I get started always helps me process what's about to go down.

3. PUMP UP THE TUNES.
At Milk Bar, we take turns playing DJ—when it's my turn, my go-tos are Tom Petty, reggae, or the Beatles. What's your favorite song to bake to?

4. MEASURE WELL AND SET THAT TIMER!
I know it's waaaaay easier to eyeball it and say your almost-filled scoop of flour is ¾ cup, but if you are skimping on all your measurements and your recipes turn out funky, don't look at me! Make sure you are filling your measuring cups and spoons all the way, without overflowing them. The same goes for watching your time; sure, you think you will know when 10 minutes is up, but why risk it? Let the timer—on your phone, oven, microwave, wristwatch, whatever—do the work.

5. TASTE AS YOU GO.
This may be the best rule and the whole reason I am a professional baker, but tasting as you go is only partly about my love of a good snack. If you wait until a recipe is completed to taste it, it will be too late to make any adjustments. So try a nibble here and there as you

whisk and mix, and correct it as you see fit—see possible fixes beginning on page 24. I know you have probably been told not to eat uncooked doughs and batters, but a couple bites won't hurt.

6. SAFETY FIRST.
Check with a grown-up before you get into a recipe. Some recipes require use of an oven, blender, or knife, which means you will need their help—ask nicely ☺. Oven mitts make a great accessory—use them *every* time you open the oven.

7. DO YOU.
Think of the recipes in this book as a framework. I've tested and measured and done the dirty work, so you can get in there and bake them as is—or you can put your personal *you*-ness into it. If you think the Berries and Cream Muffins (page 123) would be better with raspberries, get after it! Dreaming up a peanut butter cut-out cookie with chocolate glaze? INTO IT. This is your place to let loose, experiment, and explore. Let me know what you come up with!

8. (TRY TO) KEEP IT CLEAN.
I like to make a little—okay, sometimes big—mess, but I try my best to tidy up as I go. It's hard to keep your mind on

the task at hand if your area is cluttered with dirty dishes and spilled ingredients, so put things away and wipe up as you work. And the #1 rule of the kitchen is to leave your space cleaner than you found it.

9. WRITE IT DOWN.
Good bakers take notes as they go along. If you know the Choco Crunch Cookies (page 48) take 11 minutes to bake in your oven (because oven bake times can vary from one oven to another!), then make a note for your future self. This book was made to be written in, so don't be shy about marking it up.

10. SHARE.
One of my favorite things about a great baked good is the joy of sharing it. No judgments made if you want to keep all but one cookie to yourself, but I bet you can find at least one other person who needs that brilliant thing you just baked. Spread the love!

PANTRY 411

I rarely *plan* to bake. The mood or inspiration to bake strikes when I least expect it—sometimes I bolt awake with an idea I want to try out, sometimes a friend comes over and we decide to stay in and create, and other times I decide to make something last minute for a weeknight treat. Anyway, the last thing I want to do is go to the store for a ton of ingredients. The recipes in this book are based on everyday pantry items. You will not find anything that's unnecessary or hard to keep stocked in here, pinky promise. I am a firm believer in splurging on the good stuff when needed and working with the basics the rest of the time. Here are the items I like to keep in my pantry and fridge so I am always ready to bake.

NOTE: I like to play it fast and loose with creativity and imagination—that is, any kind of cookie would be happy to have some chocolate chips mixed in, am I right? But with these base ingredients, stay with the recommendations; if you swap in heavy cream for the buttermilk and your shortcakes turn out flat and flavorless, don't say I didn't warn you.

BAKING POWDER AND BAKING SODA

Baking powder and baking soda are both leaveners, but they work in different ways. Baking powder helps your cupcakes and muffins POOF up, while baking soda is responsible for helping your cookies and biscuits spread out WIDE. Both of them together help keep the texture of your baked goods light and tender, and they add a little edge to the flavor. Any brand will do—just don't use the stuff your folks keep in the fridge!

BAKING SPRAY

Sometimes called nonstick cooking spray, this oil-based spray helps your cookies, cakes, and muffins slide easily off their baking sheets or out of their baking pans. We find the spray most convenient, but you can also grease your baking sheets or pans with the slick wrapper from a stick of butter as well.

BUTTER

I. Love. Butter. So much so that I named my dog after it! These recipes will work with any standard butter (not margarine) you have on hand. Since it's good to control how much salt a recipe calls for, your best bet is to use unsalted butter. But if you have only salted butter and you are dying to get baking, you can substitute it for unsalted by applying a little math: Reduce the recipe's salt measure by ¼ teaspoon for every stick of butter used.

BUTTERMILK

Easily found in the dairy case, buttermilk adds tangy flavor and creamy richness to baked goods, AND it helps make them fluffy. If you don't have it on hand, don't sweat it: You can make your own by adding ½ tablespoon of lemon juice or white vinegar to every ½ cup of milk you need. Let it sit on the counter for 10 minutes before using. Use it right away, though!

CEREALS

One of my favorite ingredients, cereals can add flavor and texture to a recipe. Most of the time the varieties of cereal are interchangeable, so if you are more of the Fruity Pebbles type than Cocoa Krispies, do YOU!

CHOCOLATE

Though any kind of fancy chocolate will work, I'm a fan of the classic 12-ounce bag of semisweet chocolate chips, white chocolate chips, and butterscotch chips when baking at home.

COCOA POWDER

This doesn't have to be fancy. 100% cacao, unsweetened, works well. It's good to keep ol' Hershey's on hand at all times.

COCONUT

"Shredded coconut" in these recipes refers to sweetened coconut flakes, sometimes known as snowflake coconut, and you can find it easily in the baking aisle. Don't use "desiccated coconut," which is too dry and short for this use!

COOKIES

Cookies on their own are great, but cookies baked *into another* baked good or blitzed into a shake are next level. Cookies add both texture and flavor to a recipe at the same time. Baking them into other things and milkshaking are great ways to use any smashed-up cookies from the pack or not so pretty homemade ones—the sky's the limit on flavors!

CORNMEAL

Not to be confused with corn flour or cornstarch, cornmeal is ground-up dried corn kernels, and it packs a very corny punch. Any brand will work; just make sure the cornmeal is yellow.

DRINK MIXES

You probably have this killer secret ingredient in your pantry right now. Drink mixes—like lemonade, Tang, or Ovaltine— are a great way to add flavor to a recipe.

EGGS

When it says "egg" in these recipes, it means to use large eggs—basically the standard size in the store—white or brown, from the grocery store or farmers' market.

EXTRACTS

Vanilla extract is almost always my go-to flavor enhancer. Dark in color and scent, the McCormick brand will always do right by you when it comes to adding vanilla to a recipe. The recipes in this book also call for mint extract and lemon extract. These flavors are usually right next to the vanilla extract in the grocery aisle and come in handy for lots of recipes.

FLOUR

All-purpose flour is, well, for all the purposes in this cookbook. Pretty aptly named, right? Any brand will do. If you are baking gluten-free, I recommend using Cup4Cup Gluten Free flour; it works great!

FRUITS

I think nothing is better than super-fresh, in-season fruit. Strawberry shortcakes just taste better with the good stuff! Regular supermarket fruit will still turn out tasty though, so work with what you have. For smoothies, frozen fruit works great.

HEAVY CREAM

Used in biscuits and shortcakes, this might be called "whipping cream" in your grocery store. Whatever you do, do not swap it out for any kind of milk!

MARSHMALLOWS

Whether whole, toasted, or melted into some butter, marshmallows give bounce to a recipe. I like to keep one bag of mini marshmallows and a tub of Marshmallow Fluff at the ready. Lots of my favorite recipes call for them. Plus, they make an excellent snack on the fly.

MILK

Milk is obviously near and dear to my heart. When I call for "milk," I mean whole milk, though 2% or skim will work, as will dairy alternatives like soy milk or almond milk. Though they will affect the flavor a tad, you'll still be happy with the results!

NONFAT MILK POWDER

Think of nonfat milk powder as the secret weapon in the recipes that call for it. It gives an amazing depth of flavor, even though it doesn't taste so great on its own. You can find it in the aisle with powdered drink mixes or the baby food aisle of your grocery store. It's often labeled as "instant nonfat dry milk." Any brand will do. I do not recommend using it to make milk—that is the only time it loses its secret powers!

NUTS

Nuts are pretty interchangeable depending on what you love (or dislike). The same goes for nut butters. If a recipe calls for pistachios but you're really feeling pecans, swap them in! Want to make the Triple Layer Cheesecake Bars (page 30) but only have almond butter? No sweat! Pro tip: Unless you eat them a lot, store your nuts and nut butters in the fridge in airtight containers; they can get a funky flavor in the pantry over time.

OATS

Old-fashioned rolled oats are key when putting oats into a great baked good. Sadly, quick oats won't do the trick—they are made to soak up water or milk in your oatmeal in a flash, which makes them hard to bake with (they want to soak up every last drop!). Double-check the label on your oats before you start baking.

OIL

These recipes call for vegetable oil or canola oil, as they are pourable and don't have any flavor or color, which means they won't steal the show in your recipes. Grapeseed oil will also work; just avoid olive oil, coconut oil, or peanut oil, as they carry flavors of their own.

PRETZELS

Mini pretzels, not sticks, is my vote! Cute and easier to bite into, you get more flavor with them, too.

SALT

I believe every baked good needs a tiny bit of salt to bring out the flavors and keep the masterpiece balanced. Kosher salt is the fluffier cousin of normal table salt. Table salt is also often iodized, which adds an extra flavor I don't like. Diamond Crystal kosher salt is my go-to. You can find it right near the regular stuff at the grocery store. If you have only table salt or Morton brand kosher salt, that's okay—just use half the amount of salt called for in the recipes, as the grains are smaller and actually pack more salt into the measuring spoon.

SUGARS

Sugar in our world means the classic white, granulated stuff. Powdered sugar—or confectioners' sugar, as it might be labeled—is the fluffier, almost flour-like powder that's often used in frostings and sometimes to roll doughs in for a fun crackling effect. Light brown sugar is sandier, more flavorful, and—you guessed it!—brown. Pro tip: Store your brown sugar in an airtight container to keep it soft. If you've got hardened sugar on your hands, put a moist paper towel in a plastic bag along with the sugar and zap it in the microwave for 20 seconds.

TOOLS OF THE TRADE

Much like ingredients, you don't need anything super special when it comes to baking. This book is jam-packed with recipes that don't require much more than a bowl, a spoon, an oven, and definitely some imagination. Here is a roundup of a baker's basic gear. For items with an asterisk (*), ask a grown-up for help when using.

HEADSCARF

This can be a bandana, some extra ribbon, or a scarf. If you've got hair that can fall in your face, you'll need something to tie around your head to keep your hair out of your way—and to look really cool as you bake.

PANS AND BOWLS

BAKING PANS

Our MVP is the 9 by 13-inch pan. Glass, metal, or ceramic, these tall and long pans are great for cereal squares, sheet cakes, and bar cookies. We like an 8-inch square pan for some smaller recipes, too. Feel free to halve a recipe that calls for a 9 by 13-inch rectangular pan if all you have is an 8-inch square one.

BAKING SHEETS

When we say "baking sheet" we (and basically everyone else) mean half-sheet pans—that is, a pan that is 18 inches by 13 inches. The ones with a heavy bottom ensure that your cookies will bake evenly. You should have two or three baking sheets ready to rock.

LOAF PAN

There are often variations in the dimensions of a 1-pound loaf pan—some are 8½ inches long whereas others are 9 inches long. These recipes work in all loaf pans labeled "1 pound." Glass, ceramic, or metal all work fine.

MIXING BOWLS

While mixing bowls come in all sizes, use a bigger bowl than you think necessary. Trust me, it's cleaner this way. And remember: Only glass or ceramic in the microwave!

NONSTICK PAN

A large frying pan with a nonstick coating is key for making sure your pancakes are easy to flip.

HAND TOOLS

FORK

You would be surprised how much can be done with this simple tool. It's great for whisking together dry ingredients, smooshing veggies into a Veggie Frittata Bite (page 81), or drizzling chocolate onto an extra-large cookie (google "Jackson Pollock" when you have a chance).

KNIVES*

Most of the ingredients that require prepping in this book are soft enough to be cut with a butter knife, but some of the items like bars or extra-large cookies may require a sharper knife. Ask a grown-up for help!

MEASURING CUPS AND SPOONS

You'll put these to good use— for measuring ingredients, portioning cupcake batter into pans, or scooping out dough for cookies. Just make sure you have a range from ¼ cup to 1 cup for the cup measurements, and ⅛ teaspoon to 1 tablespoon for the spoon measurements.

SCOOPS: ICE CREAM SCOOP/COOKIE SCOOP

The secret to making sure cookies come out amazing every time is using a 2-tablespoon cookie scoop. You can find them at most stores or on Amazon; OXO makes our favorite. And ice cream scoops are great for building a perfect milkshake or getting a well-rounded ice cream topper for your chocolate waffle.

SPATULAS, RUBBER AND PLASTIC

A sturdy "rubber" (or usually, silicone) spatula is a necessity for scraping down the sides of a mixing bowl, transferring batters to baking pans, and licking up the last bits of frosting. They come in all colors and sizes—you can never have too many.

TIMER

Whether it's on the microwave or on a phone, you are going to need a timer for everything that goes into the oven. We strongly support obnoxious ringtones cued up on an iPhone.

TOOTHPICKS

Your BFF for testing the doneness of cakes, muffins, and breads is a wooden toothpick. Before you take the baked item out of the oven, stick a 'pick in the center and pull it out. See page 23 for our key.

WHISK

The best tool for mixing ingredients, a whisk ensures that everything you mix is combined realllly well. A medium whisk works great.

WOODEN SPOON

A plain-Jane wooden spoon is key for smooshing together wet and dry ingredients.

HEAVY EQUIPMENT

BLENDER

One of the most fun things to use in the kitchen, blenders can have a wide variety of features. For the recipes in this book, keep it simple: If it blends, it will work. Just make sure you put the top on.

FRIDGE/FREEZER

I am not the most patient person, so when I make a triple-layer cheesecake, I want to slice into it as quickly as possible. But from time to time I will suggest you stash your treats in the fridge or freezer to chill first, or recommend you store them in the fridge after they are done to help them last as long as possible; if it's really cold outside, you can put them out there, too!

MICROWAVE

You can use a microwave for everything from softening and melting butter or chocolate to making Rice Krispie treats. Though it is one of humanity's greatest inventions, every microwave is different. Our recipes suggest you use 15- or 30-second bursts of heat, but even still, keep your eye on the butter or chocolate—these items can overheat or burn quickly when left unattended!

MIXER, STAND OR HAND, WITH ATTACHMENTS

Most of the recipes in this book can be mixed with a wooden spoon and some muscle. But if you have a stand mixer fitted with the paddle and whisk attachments, don't be afraid to use it. A handheld electric granny mixer will also work. (I still use my grandma's, hence the name.)

OVEN

Did you know that, much like microwaves, every oven is different? If you swear you are doing everything right and your treats are still not coming out as planned, your oven may be to blame; see page 24 for solutions.

OVEN MITTS

Padded and always there when you need them, these kitchen MVPs will keep your hands safe. Don't even THINK about going near the oven without 'em. You are going to be using these pals often, so you might as well get a color or design that brings you joy!

WAFFLE MAKER

If you are a waffle fan, raise your hand. Waffles are a breeze to make at home, and today's machines cost typically less than $20—ask for one for your next birthday, if you don't already have one!

MEASURING 101: WETS, DRIES, AND DONENESS

I've said it before and I will say it again: *Measuring well is key in baking.* I have taken all the guesswork out of these recipes by measuring and remeasuring, testing and retesting, until they are just right. Now it is up to you to take it on home! Here is how to get it done:

MEASURING DRY INGREDIENTS

Use the right size measuring cup to scoop out your flour, sugar, brown sugar, powdered sugar, cocoa powder, or cornmeal, and fill the cup to the top. Then run the back of your hand or a butter knife along the top of the cup to level off any extra.

For brown sugar

This brown-eyed babe is fluffier than white sugar, so to measure it correctly, you've gotta make sure it's packed tightly in the cup before leveling off the top. (You're in business if you dump your brown sugar into the bowl and it keeps the shape of its measuring cup.)

For baking powder, baking soda, or salt

Stick with measuring spoons instead. Remember, tablespoons are the big guys and teaspoons are the babies! You use the spoons just as you would the cup measures: Fill the spoon with the ingredient and use your finger to level off any extra (your measurements should go right up to the lip of the spoon or cup).

MEASURING WET INGREDIENTS

Clear measuring cups are great for determining the right amount of liquids, like milk, heavy cream, buttermilk, or juice. Just put the measuring cup on the counter, bend down so you are level with the measuring cup, then pour the liquid in until it hits the line that matches the amount you want to measure. Boom!

For smaller amounts of wet ingredients

For measuring extracts, lemon juice, splashes of milk, and the like, stick to your measuring spoons. Friendly reminder: Tablespoons are the big guys and teaspoons are the babies!

Measuring butter

Some wonderful genius at Butter HQ long ago decided to mark the butter wrappers with handy 1-tablespoon lines to save us from having to measure—thank you, Butter Boss! One full stick of butter is 8 tablespoons (aka, ½ cup, or ¼ pound).

Measuring by the bag/jar/can

Every so often the ingredients list says to use a full bag of something—say, marshmallows or chocolate chips, or a jar of jam or a can of corn. The recipe says what size bag or jar or can is needed, so check to see that yours has the same number of ounces before you dump it in.

THE TOOTHPICK METHOD

If I could have one superpower, it would be X-ray vision. Sure, flying would be fun, and superhuman strength could help me open pickle jars. But X-ray vision would mean I could read my sister's diary, watch movies without having to buy a ticket, and—especially—peek inside my baked goods to see if they are done or not. Alas, I have to use a less X-Men way of determining if the cakes, muffins, and loaves are ready to come out of the oven: the toothpick method.

It's super simple: You stick a clean toothpick into the center of your baked good, pull it out, and examine it. You're looking for the toothpick to come out clean (see the "Ready!" toothpick pictured below), telling you that the crumb is fully set and no extra moisture is left over. A clean toothpick means the item will slice well and not crumble when you eat it. If the toothpick is wet, back in the oven it goes!

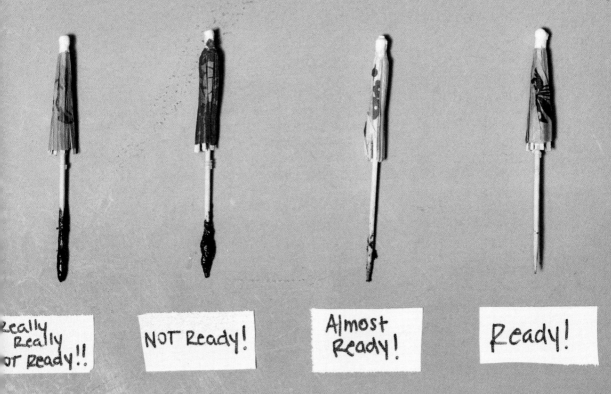

Really Really ot Ready!!

NOT Ready!

Almost Ready!

Ready!

HELP HOTLINE!

No one is perfect; I'm sure not. If you're trying your best but keep running into issues with a recipe, there may be a larger problem. Worry not; I have made every mistake in the book, and I am here to share my solutions with you!

PROBLEM: *Something (anything) weird is going on.*
SOLUTION: Always start with rereading the recipe, line by line, and making sure that you've added all the ingredients and followed all the instructions. Sometimes I can catch my own mistakes this way!

PROBLEM: *You are not sure if your dough is right . . . or you're baking in a new kitchen for the first time.*
SOLUTION: Bake one cookie (or cupcake, muffin, pancake, etc.) from your batch on its own, before committing to the whole shebang. This will let you test-drive your batter and the oven, learning any of its quirks before it is too late—is it baking too fast, or too slow? This will allow you to adjust the batter or the bake time (or know if it might be worth starting over!).

PROBLEM: *Your cookies are burning on the bottom, but raw on the top—or vice versa.*
SOLUTION: Your oven rack may be too low or too high, depending on whether the heat in your oven comes from the bottom or the top. Try moving the rack up or down a notch with the help of an adult.

PROBLEM: *One side of your cookies is burning and the other side is perfect.*
SOLUTION: Your oven may be uneven. It happens! Set a timer for halfway through your bake time, and use oven mitts to rotate your pan so the fronts of your cookies are now in the back.

PROBLEM: *No matter what you do, when the timer goes off your cookies are burnt.*
SOLUTION: Your oven might be a hothead! Test the real temperature of your oven with an oven thermometer, then adjust your oven temperature accordingly. Oven thermometers are available at most grocery stores or on Amazon.com.

PROBLEM: *Your cookies are dissolving into a puddle in the oven.*
SOLUTION: This is a dough issue. If your dough is exceptionally wet when you mix it—if it looks really shiny or oily—your butter was likely too hot. Throw it in the fridge for a few minutes to firm it up before you do the scooping and baking. Then test one cookie and make sure it's baking the way you want! If the cookies are still baking strangely, try remaking the recipe.

PROBLEM: *Your cupcakes and muffins are sinking in the middle.*

SOLUTION: You are probably opening and closing the oven too much. I know it's hard to be patient, but try to use the oven light to spy on your treats, instead of opening the door. Opening the door lets cold air in and hot air out! But if this still isn't doing the trick, add more oven time! It's possible that the center of your muffin or cupcake is underbaked.

PROBLEM: *I can't taste the mint/lemon/vanilla.*

SOLUTION: Up your extract! Extracts vary in intensity, so you may be working with a weaker one. Increase your flavor by adding ¼ teaspoon more of extract—just don't get too wild, as this also adds liquid to the mix.

PROBLEM: *My shake/quake/ smoothie is too thick/too thin.*

SOLUTION: These babes are a dealer's choice on thickness. If you want something slurpable, add more milk or juice to the blender, or blend it a bit longer; if you like to get a spoon involved, keep your liquids minimal and blend it less.

PROBLEM: *The recipe came out too salty/sweet.*

SOLUTION: First, double-check your butter! All the recipes call for unsalted butter, so if you used the salted kind, the result would be saltier tasting. Then, check your measurements; with salt and sugar, the difference between ¼ teaspoon and ½ teaspoon, or ¼ cup and ½ cup, is a lot (it's double!), so make sure you're using the correct measurements. Then, check the kind of salt you're using (see page 19). Our recipes call for kosher salt, and we prefer the Diamond Crystal brand. If you are using Morton kosher salt or regular table salt, you'll need to use only about half the amount of salt. If your goodies are too sweet, you may need to bring the sugar down (start with subtracting a tablespoon next time you make it) or bring the salt up slightly—try adding ⅛ teaspoon to start.

PROBLEM: *I am whipping and whipping and my frosting is still wet.*

SOLUTION 1: You may have added the liquids or fruit to the frosting too early, and the butter–sugar mixture may not have had enough time to warm up! Take out one-third of the frosting from your mixing bowl and microwave it (I know!) for 30 seconds, then add it to the bowl and keep mixing. Your frosting should improve!

SOLUTION 2: You may have mismeasured the liquid in the frosting recipe. Add more powdered sugar, or start a new batch and be extra careful to check the milk amount and measuring spoons for accuracy.

PROBLEM: *I want beautiful sugar cookies, but my glazes aren't much to look at.*

SOLUTION: Add in a drop at a time of food coloring to get your desired color, but try to match the color to the flavor at hand—no offense, blue raspberry! If your glaze came out too thin, whisk in some more powdered sugar.

CHOCOLATE CUT-OUT COOKIES

FYI
Chilling the dough makes it easier to roll out, *plus* you can easily stash a bag of dough in the fridge for later.

Makes 24 cookies, depending on cut-out size

Vanilla cut-out cookies are classic, and gingerbread is everywhere you look in December, but where is the love for chocolate? These cocoa-packed shapes are third fiddle to no one, my friends—plus the glaze combinations are endless!

INGREDIENTS

1 egg

½ teaspoon vanilla extract

1⅔ cups flour, plus more for dusting

1 cup powdered sugar

⅓ cup cocoa powder

½ teaspoon kosher salt

1½ sticks (12 tablespoons) unsalted butter, melted

EQUIPMENT

2 BAKING SHEETS

BAKING SPRAY

MIXING BOWLS

MEASURING CUPS + SPOONS

WHISK

WOODEN SPOON

3 ZIP-TOP PLASTIC BAGS (OR PLASTIC WRAP)

FRIDGE

OVEN

ROLLING PIN

RULER

COOKIE CUTTERS

PLASTIC SPATULA

OVEN MITTS

PREP!

Coat the baking sheets with baking spray.

WHISK AND COMBINE!

In a small bowl, whisk together the egg and vanilla. In a large bowl, combine the flour, powdered sugar, cocoa powder, and salt with a wooden spoon. Mix in the egg mixture. Add the butter and stir until smooth. It may be easiest to ditch the spoon and use your hands to form the dough.

SHAPE AND CHILL!

Form the dough into a ball, and divide the ball into 3 pieces. Place each piece into a plastic bag. Pat the dough smooth and flatten with your hands. Refrigerate the bags for 15 minutes. Meanwhile, preheat the oven to 350°F.

ROLL AND CUT!

Dust a clean, dry section of your countertop with a little flour. Take a piece of dough and place it on the counter. Dust the rolling pin with a little flour and roll out the dough until it is ¼ inch thick

(use a ruler!). Use cookie cutters to cut shapes. Using a spatula, lift the shapes and transfer them to the prepared baking sheets. Repeat with the remaining dough. If you use a range of cookie cutter sizes and shapes, keep the bigger cut-outs on one baking sheet and the smaller on the other baking sheet.

BAKE!

Bake the cookies at 350°F for 6 to 12 minutes). Double-check that you set the timer (6 minutes for smaller, 12 minutes for larger cookies). Because these cookies are already dark brown, it's tricky to tell by sight when they're ready to take out of the oven. The timer is your best friend! With oven mitts, remove the baking sheets from the oven and cool the cookies completely on the baking sheets.

MAKE IT YOUR OWN!

Ready to get your Picasso on? Turn to page 144 to see our fave way to decorate!

FYI
If you have leftover scraps of dough after you cut out your cookies, combine them into a ball and roll out the ball anew for more cookies.

FRENCH TOAST MUFFINS

Makes 6 muffins

I LOVE French toast. But there is one flaw: You can make only one or two at a time, and I love having people over for breakfast, especially when it's cold out. So I thought, "How do I create French toast I can make a bunch of at a time?" And then I figured, "And what if I could hold it in my hand?" What better way to impress on a cozy, winter morning than to pack all the gooey, cinnamony amazingness of French toast into a batch of muffins? Bonus points for dressing it up with butter and maple syrup! And bacon on the side? Your call.

BTW
This is a fantastic way to use up those last pieces of bread that may be a little stale.

INGREDIENTS

3 eggs

¾ cup milk

⅓ cup light brown sugar

¼ cup flour

½ teaspoon vanilla extract

¼ teaspoon ground cinnamon

¼ teaspoon kosher salt

6 slices white bread

SERVING

Unsalted butter

Maple syrup

EQUIPMENT
OVEN
BAKING SPRAY
6- OR 12-CUP CUPCAKE/MUFFIN PAN
MIXING BOWL
MEASURING CUPS + SPOONS
WHISK
RUBBER SPATULA
OVEN MITTS

PREP!
Preheat the oven to 375°F. Spray 6 cups of a muffin pan (no liners required!).

WHISK!
In a large bowl, whisk together the eggs, milk, brown sugar, flour, vanilla, cinnamon, and salt until well combined.

RIP IT!
Tear the bread slices into 1-inch pieces, as if you were feeding ducks in the park, and submerge them in the egg mixture. Make sure they are fully coated.

SCOOP!
Using a measuring cup, scoop ⅓ cup of the batter into each of the 6 prepared cups in the muffin pan. The batter will be almost level with the top edge of the cup (but it shouldn't go over!). Look through and make sure the gooey bread pieces are divided as evenly as possible among the muffin cups—move some around if you need to.

BAKE!
Bake the muffins at 375°F for 25 minutes. Add a couple more minutes if you'd like your French toast a little toastier! Double-check that you set your timer for these muffins; it will be hard to tell visually when they are ready. With oven mitts, take the muffin pan out of the oven.

SERVE!
Let the muffins cool for 2 minutes, then pop them out of the pan and serve warm on plates, with the butter and maple syrup.

These are best eaten fresh out of the oven. Bake and eat these babes immediately—they aren't as awesome on day 2.

TRIPLE LAYER CHEESECAKE BARS

Makes 24 layered squares

Like a labradoodle or a Crunchwrap Supreme, some of the best inventions are really just two amazing things smooshed together. Pizza bagels! Pool slides! Sporks! Mermaids! Keytars! If we know that two amazing things smooshed together are awesome, *three* amazing things together must be *out of control*! They are. Cheesecake, peanut butter cheesecake, and chocolate cheesecake. The power of three, my friends.

EQUIPMENT

OVEN

9 BY 13-INCH BAKING PAN

BAKING SPRAY

MIXING BOWLS

MEASURING CUPS + SPOONS

WOODEN SPOON

WHISK

RUBBER SPATULA

OVEN MITTS

FRIDGE OR FREEZER (OPTIONAL)

BUTTER KNIFE

INGREDIENTS

FOR THE CRUST

18 whole graham crackers, crushed into crumbs (or 3 cups graham crumbs)

1 stick (8 tablespoons) unsalted butter, melted

¼ cup sugar

¼ teaspoon kosher salt

FOR THE CHEESECAKE LAYERS

4 (8-ounce) packages cream cheese, softened

½ cup sugar

3 eggs

2 teaspoons vanilla extract

2 tablespoons flour

½ teaspoon kosher salt

⅔ cup chocolate chips, melted

½ cup peanut butter

PREP!

Preheat the oven to 325°F and coat the baking pan with baking spray.

COMBINE AND PRESS!

Stir together the graham cracker crumbs, butter, ¼ cup sugar, and the salt, mixing until well combined. Using your hands, press this mixture into the bottom of your prepared pan, smooshing to make an even layer that fills in to all the corners.

MIX AND WHISK!

In a large bowl, use a wooden spoon to mix the cream cheese and ½ cup sugar until smooth. Switch to a whisk and add the eggs and vanilla, whisking until smooth. Whisk in the flour and ½ teaspoon salt until well combined.

FLAVOR THE LAYERS!

Divide the batter into 3 small bowls. Add the melted chocolate to one of the batter bowls and mix until well combined. Add the peanut butter to another of the batter bowls and mix until well combined. Keep the third bowl as is.

LAYER UP!

Pour your chocolate batter on top of the crumb crust in the pan and use a spatula to spread it evenly. Pour your peanut butter batter on top of the chocolate and use the spatula to spread it evenly. Finally, pour your plain batter onto the peanut butter batter layer and spread it evenly.

BAKE!

Bake at 325°F for 30 to 35 minutes, until the center sets and does not jiggle when you shake the pan. Using oven mitts, remove the pan from the oven and let cool completely. (I like to pop my pan in the fridge or freezer to speed this up.) Cut the baked bars into 4 rows down the length and 6 rows across. Store in an airtight container in the fridge for up to 2 weeks.

COCO CABANA CEREAL SQUARES

FYI
The marshmallows will balloon up in a hilarious way when you microwave them, so make sure you use an oversize bowl.

Makes 15 squares

One of my favorite ways to combat the dreary, sludgy winter blues is to blast the Beach Boys, break out my flip-flops and favorite Hawaiian shirt, turn the heat up in my apartment, and snack on something tropical. There is absolutely no reason the weather has to ruin a perfectly good beach day; these coconut-studded, fruity cereal squares will bring all the sunshine you need. Just don't forget the SPF 50.

INGREDIENTS

5 tablespoons unsalted butter (save the paper it's wrapped in!)

1 (10.5-ounce) bag marshmallows

1½ cups sweetened shredded coconut

8 cups Froot Loops cereal

BTW
Swap the cereal for whatever you love most (or whatever you've got in the cupboard)!

PREP!
Coat the baking pan with baking spray.

MELT!
In a very large microwave-safe bowl, melt the butter and marshmallows together for 2 minutes. Remove from the microwave and stir, then microwave for 1 more minute. Stir until smooth.

ADD MIX-INS!
Add the coconut to the marshmallow mixture and stir with a spatula until every bit is coated.

CEREAL TIME!
Add the Froot Loops to the marshmallow mixture and mix until every bit is coated.

SPREAD AND COOL!
Scrape the mixture into the prepared pan and spread evenly with a greased spatula or with the butter paper (my grandma taught me this!). Let cool until firm, 15 to 20 minutes, then cut into 3 lengthwise rows and 5 crosswise rows to make 15 treats. Store in an airtight container on your counter for up to 5 days.

EQUIPMENT

9 BY 13-INCH BAKING PAN

BAKING SPRAY

MICROWAVE + LARGE MICROWAVE-
   SAFE BOWL

RUBBER SPATULA

BUTTER KNIFE

BUILDING BLOCKS COOKIE SANDWICHES

Makes 24 cookie sandwiches

My house always had a strict "Don't play with your food" rule, which stopped me from blowing bubbles in my chocolate milk or pretending that my spaghetti was a fancy new wig. After years of fighting my urge to goof off with my meals, I made these building block cookies as the ultimate revenge. These rule-breaking chocolate-on-chocolate sandwich cookies are the perfect playtime companion when you've misplaced all your LEGOs.* And the cleanup time is much more delicious.

* Check under the couch; that's where mine always end up!

1 batch (48) chocolate cut-out cookies (recipe follows), made with 1 by 2-inch rectangle cutters

1 batch (2 cups) dark chocolate frosting (recipe follows)

1 cup sprinkles or colored sanding sugar

STACK!

Arrange the cookies on a counter. Swirl a 2-tablespoon dollop of frosting on the bottom of one of the cookies. Smooth it with the back of a dinner spoon to make an even layer. Top it with another cookie and press together, squeezing just until the frosting oozes to the edge of the cookie. Repeat with the remaining cookies and frosting.

SPRINKLE AND ROLL!

Spread the sprinkles or colored sanding sugar on a plate. Turning a cookie on its side, roll the outer edge of the cookie in the sprinkles, letting the decoration get stuck to the oozing frosting. Set the cookie on a plate. Repeat with the remaining cookies. Store in an airtight container on the counter for up to 1 week or in the freezer for up to 1 month; they're pretty awesome frozen!

(recipe continues)

CHOCOLATE CUT-OUT COOKIES

Makes 48 cookies

INGREDIENTS

1 egg

½ teaspoon vanilla extract

1⅔ cups flour, plus more for dusting

1 cup powdered sugar

⅓ cup cocoa powder

½ teaspoon kosher salt

1½ sticks (12 tablespoons) unsalted butter, melted

EQUIPMENT

2 BAKING SHEETS

BAKING SPRAY

MIXING BOWLS

MEASURING CUPS + SPOONS

WHISK

WOODEN SPOON

3 ZIP-TOP PLASTIC BAGS (OR PLASTIC WRAP)

FRIDGE

OVEN

ROLLING PIN

RULER

SQUIGGLE-EDGED PASTRY ROLLER

PLASTIC SPATULA

OVEN MITTS

PREP!

Coat your baking sheets with baking spray.

WHISK AND COMBINE!

In a small bowl, whisk together the egg and vanilla. In a large bowl, combine the flour, powdered sugar, cocoa powder, and salt with a wooden spoon. Mix in the egg mixture. Add the butter and stir until smooth. It may be easiest to ditch the spoon and use your hands to form the dough.

SHAPE AND CHILL!

Form the dough into a ball, and divide the ball into 3 pieces. Place each piece into a plastic bag and pat the dough smooth to flatten with your hands. Refrigerate the bags for 15 minutes. Meanwhile, preheat the oven to 350°F.

ROLL AND CUT!

Dust a clean, dry section of your countertop with a little flour. Take a piece of dough out of the plastic bag and place on the counter. Dust the rolling pin with a little flour and roll out the dough until it is a rectangle that is ¼ inch thick (use a ruler!). Using a squiggle-edged pastry roller, cut your dough into 2 lengthwise rows and 8 crosswise rows. Repeat with the remaining 2 packages of dough, for 48 cookies total. Use a spatula to lift the rectangles of dough and transfer them to your prepared baking sheets.

FYI

Chilling the dough in the fridge for 15 minutes makes it easier to roll out, *plus* you can easily stash a bag of dough for later baking. If you have leftover scraps of dough after you cut out your cookies, combine them into a ball and roll it out anew for even more cookies. (If the dough gets too sticky, chill it in the fridge again.)

DARK CHOCOLATE FROSTING

Makes 2 cups

BAKE!

Bake the cookies at 350°F for 6 to 8 minutes. Double-check that you set the timer. Because these cookies are already dark brown from the cocoa, it's tricky to tell by sight when they are ready to take out of the oven. With oven mitts, remove the baking sheets from the oven and cool the cookies completely on the baking sheets.

INGREDIENTS

1½ sticks (12 tablespoons) unsalted butter, softened

2¼ cups powdered sugar

⅓ cup cocoa powder

3 tablespoons milk

¾ teaspoon vanilla extract

¼ teaspoon kosher salt

MIX!

Starting on low speed, use the mixer to combine your butter, powdered sugar, and cocoa powder. Beat for 1 minute, then increase the mixer speed to medium and beat until super smooth, about 3 minutes. Turn off the mixer. Use your spatula to scrape down the sides of your bowl well.

ADD AND FLUFF!

Add the milk, vanilla, and salt to the bowl. Continue mixing until combined and fluffy, about 1 minute.

EQUIPMENT

HAND MIXER OR STAND MIXER WITH
    PADDLE ATTACHMENT

MIXING BOWL

MEASURING CUPS + SPOONS

RUBBER SPATULA

DINNER SPOON

COMPOST PANCAKES

Makes 6 to 8 pancakes

The Compost Cookie—a vanilla cookie jam-packed with oats, pretzels, potato chips, graham cracker crumbs, coffee, and studded with chocolate and butterscotch chips—has been a crowd-pleaser at Milk Bar since we first opened our doors in 2008. After many an early A.M. in the bakery, we found out these flavors and textures make a great pancake, too—with a cup of coffee as an option on the side for the really sleepy grown-ups!

FYI
Use any mixture of your favorite sweet and salty foods from the pantry. That's the spirit of these pancakes!

INGREDIENTS

1 cup flour

2 tablespoons sugar

1 tablespoon + 1 teaspoon baking powder

1 teaspoon kosher salt

¾ cup milk

1 egg

3 tablespoons vegetable oil

8 snack-size pretzels, crumbled

¼ cup old-fashioned rolled oats

½ cup crumbled graham crackers

¼ cup chocolate chips

¼ cup butterscotch chips

SERVING
Unsalted butter

Maple syrup

EQUIPMENT
MIXING BOWLS

MEASURING CUPS + SPOONS

WHISK

BAKING SPRAY

NONSTICK PAN OR GRIDDLE

PLASTIC SPATULA

WHISK THE DRY!
In a medium bowl, whisk together the flour, sugar, baking powder, and salt.

WHISK THE WET AND COMBINE!
In a small bowl, whisk together the milk, egg, and oil. Pour this into the flour mixture and whisk until your pancake batter is mostly smooth.

ADD MIX-INS!
In a medium bowl, combine the pretzels, oats, graham crackers, chocolate chips, and butterscotch chips.

COOK!
Spray your nonstick pan or griddle with baking spray and warm it over medium heat. Pour ¼ cup of the batter onto the prepared pan or griddle. Then sprinkle 3 tablespoons of your pretzel/chocolate chip mixture on top! Cook until the pancake batter has set on the bottom and browned (bubbles will begin to appear on the top and a few will burst), 1 to 2 minutes. Flip carefully with the spatula and cook the other side until golden brown, 1 to 2 minutes more. Remove the pancake from the pan or griddle using the spatula and keep warm while you make the remaining pancakes.

SERVE!
Serve warm with some butter and maple syrup.

BERRY LOCO CUPCAKES

Makes 12 frosted cupcakes

When you're coconuts for someone special, and you are berry excited to show it, these cupcakes are just the ticket. Little coconut-flavored cakes with a sweet raspberry frosting are already something you're guaranteed to like, and the raspberries turn the frosting an electric shade of pink, which is the universal color of L-O-V-E, whether it's for your BFF, your mom or pop, or your next-door neighbor, crush, or soul mate.

1 batch (12) coconut cupcakes (recipe follows)

1 batch (2 cups) raspberry frosting (recipe follows)

ASSEMBLE!

Place the cupcakes on the countertop. Dollop a large spoonful of strawberry frosting on top of each cupcake—about 2 tablespoons' worth. Use the back side of a spoon to smooth your frosting into an even and fluffy layer. Serve the same day you frost the cupcakes!

(recipe continues)

COCONUT CUPCAKES

Makes 12 cupcakes

FYI
These are best eaten fresh out of the oven. Bake and eat these babes immediately—they aren't as awesome on day 2.

INGREDIENTS

1¼ cups flour

1 tablespoon baking powder

¾ teaspoon kosher salt

½ stick (4 tablespoons) unsalted butter, melted

¾ cup sugar

3 tablespoons light brown sugar

2 eggs

½ cup vegetable oil

1 teaspoon vanilla extract

⅔ cup buttermilk

1 cup sweetened flaked coconut

PREP!

Preheat the oven to 350°F. Line the cupcake pan with the cupcake liners.

MIX THE DRY!

In a large bowl, combine the flour, baking powder, and salt.

WHISK THE WET AND COMBINE!

In a medium bowl, whisk together the butter, both sugars, and eggs until well combined. Whisk in the oil and vanilla. Whisk in the buttermilk. Whisk your wet ingredients into the dry ingredients until smooth. Stir in the coconut.

SCOOP AND BAKE!

Use a ¼-cup measure to scoop portions of the batter into the cupcake cups. The batter will be almost level with the top edge of the liner (but it shouldn't go over!). Bake at 350°F for 15 to 20 minutes, until the tops brown slightly and a toothpick comes out clean when poked into the center of a cupcake (see page 23). Using oven mitts, remove the cupcakes from the oven and cool them completely in the pan.

FYI
If you don't have buttermilk, you can DIY your own by combining ⅔ cup milk with 2 teaspoons lemon juice or white vinegar, and letting it sit on the counter for 10 minutes. Use immediately!

EQUIPMENT

OVEN

12-CUP CUPCAKE/MUFFIN PAN

12 PAPER CUPCAKE LINERS

MIXING BOWLS

MEASURING CUPS + SPOONS

WHISK

RUBBER SPATULA

TOOTHPICK

OVEN MITTS

RASPBERRY FROSTING

Makes 2 cups

INGREDIENTS

1½ sticks (12 tablespoons) unsalted butter

2¼ cups powdered sugar

12 fresh raspberries (about ¾ cup)

¼ teaspoon kosher salt

MIX!

Starting on low speed, use the mixer to combine the butter and sugar for 1 minute. Increase to medium speed and whip until super smooth, about 3 minutes. Turn off the mixer. Use the spatula to scrape down the sides of the bowl well.

ADD AND FLUFF!

Add the fresh raspberries and salt. Continue mixing until combined and fluffy, about 1 minute.

FYI
This frosting is *out of this world*! Only thing: You have to serve it the day you make it!

EQUIPMENT

HAND MIXER OR STAND MIXER WITH
   PADDLE ATTACHMENT

LARGE MIXING BOWL

MEASURING CUPS + SPOONS

RUBBER SPATULA

DINNER SPOON

SNOW ICE CREAM

Makes 2 servings

If you thought a snowman was the most epic thing you could make with some fresh snow, listen up. Frosty ain't got nothing on this creamy, easy, DIY ice cream. Best consumed inside an epic snow fort.

INGREDIENTS

1 cup milk or heavy cream

⅓ cup sugar

1 teaspoon vanilla extract

4 cups snow, fluffy and clean

MIX!

In a medium bowl, whisk together the milk, sugar, and vanilla.

SCOOP!

Make 1 mound of snow in each of 2 medium bowls. Don't pack the snow too much; you want it nice and fluffy.

POUR AND EAT UP!

Pour your sweet, creamy mixture over the bowls of fresh snow and eat—immediately!

A trillion trillion snowflakes fall every year

Snowflakes always have six sides

The largest snow fort ever was in Finland: more than 20,000 square meters

The largest snowflake ever was 15 inches wide

Monkeys have snowball fights, too!

The biggest snowball fight ever was in Seattle—more than 5,834 ballers!

EQUIPMENT

MIXING BOWLS

MEASURING CUPS + SPOONS

WHISK

ICE CREAM/COOKIE SCOOP

GERMAN CHOCOLATE CAKE WAFFLES

Makes 3 waffles

One of my favorite dinnertimes is "international night." We select our menu by spinning the globe, closing our eyes, and landing a finger on a random country. I admit that I have peeked once or twice to land on Germany as an excuse to make these waffles for dinner. I am not sure what exactly makes the combination of chocolate, coconut, and pecan German, but I do know when the waffles hit the table, everyone says "Ja, bitte!" ("Yes, please!").

FEBRUARY

FYI
Don't worry about smoothing your batter to cover the whole surface of your waffle maker; it will spread out as it cooks!

INGREDIENTS

1 cup flour

½ cup cocoa powder

½ cup sugar

1 tablespoon + 1 teaspoon baking powder

1 teaspoon kosher salt

¾ cup milk

1 egg

3 tablespoons vegetable oil

⅓ cup sweetened shredded coconut

SERVING

Butter pecan ice cream

EQUIPMENT

WAFFLE MAKER

MIXING BOWLS

MEASURING CUPS + SPOONS

WHISK

PLASTIC SPATULA

ICE CREAM/COOKIE SCOOP

PREP!

Turn on the waffle maker and set it to medium heat.

WHISK THE DRY!

In a medium bowl, whisk together the flour, cocoa powder, sugar, baking powder, and salt.

WHISK THE WET AND COMBINE!

In a small bowl, whisk together the milk, egg, and oil. Pour this milk mixture into the flour mixture and whisk until the pancake batter is mostly smooth. Stir in the coconut.

FYI
I love butter pecan, but any ice cream will do!

COOK AND SERVE!

Pour ½ cup of the batter—or the amount your waffle maker suggests—into the middle of the waffle maker, smoothing it slightly. Close and cook for about 2 minutes, or until cooked through. Lift out the waffle using the spatula, place it on a plate, and serve right away with a heaping scoop of ice cream. Make the remaining 2 waffles the same way.

GERMAN 101

Ja: Yes

Danke: Thank you

Guten Morgen: Good morning

Katze: Cat

Hund: Dog

Eiscreme: Ice cream

CHOCO CRUNCH COOKIES

Makes 18 to 24 cookies

FYI
The secret ingredient in these cookies is the milk powder; read up on it on page 19.

Of course, cereal is good for breakfast. No one is arguing that fact. But if you are only having cereal with a bowl and spoon in the morning, you are not living life, my friend. Cereal can be mixed with marshmallows and butter for a gooey snack—see page 33, for example—or, even crazier, folded into cookie dough to give you some crunch to go with the gooey marshmallow in these cookies. Once you see cereal as a daylong option, the rest of your life begins.

INGREDIENTS

1½ cups flour

¼ cup cocoa powder

2 tablespoons nonfat milk powder

1¼ teaspoons kosher salt

½ teaspoon baking powder

¼ teaspoon baking soda

2 sticks (16 tablespoons) unsalted butter, super soft

¾ cup packed light brown sugar

½ cup sugar

1 egg

2 teaspoons vanilla extract

1 cup Cocoa Krispies cereal

1 cup chocolate chips

1 cup mini marshmallows

EQUIPMENT

OVEN

2 BAKING SHEETS

BAKING SPRAY

MIXING BOWLS

MEASURING CUPS + SPOONS

WOODEN SPOON

ICE CREAM/COOKIE SCOOP

OVEN MITTS

PREP!

Preheat the oven to 350°F. Coat the baking sheets with baking spray.

MIX THE DRY!

In a medium bowl, mix the flour, cocoa powder, milk powder, salt, baking powder, and baking soda.

MIX THE WET AND COMBINE!

In a large bowl, and using a wooden spoon, mix the butter and both sugars, flexing your muscles for about 2 minutes, until everything is fully combined. Add the egg and vanilla and stir until combined and fluffy, about 1 minute.

Add the dry mixture to the wet mixture, mixing until just combined.

ADD MIX-INS!

Fold in the Cocoa Krispies, chocolate chips, and marshmallows.

SCOOP AND BAKE!

Scoop your dough into balls that are about 2 tablespoons in size and place them 2 to 3 inches apart on the prepared baking sheets. Bake the cookies at 350°F for 10 to 12 minutes. Double-check that you set the timer; these cookies are already dark brown, so it's tricky to tell by sight when they're ready to take out of the oven. The timer is your best friend! Using oven mitts, remove the baking sheets from the oven and cool the cookies completely on the baking sheets. Store the cooled cookies in an airtight container for up to 1 week.

NOTE: You want your butter to be soft and melty, not fully liquid and definitely not steaming hot. The best way to do this is to soften it in the microwave (in a microwave-safe bowl) on high for 30 seconds. If you need to heat it longer (some microwaves are stronger than others), do it in 15-second bursts, and take a look at it between zaps.

FYI
If you're not into the gooey parts of this cookie, remove the mini marshmallows— no worries!

FYI
If you like a smaller (or larger) cookie, go for it—you're the boss, after all! Keep in mind that a smaller scoop will bake faster (reduce the bake time by 2 to 4 minutes) and a larger scoop will bake longer (increase the bake time by 2 to 4 minutes).

COOKIE TIPS

When it comes to baking cookies, there are some tried-and-true practices that will guarantee cookie perfection every time.

· **Use a scoop.** A 2-tablespoon cookie scoop is easy to come by and will help you make your cookies the same size, which means they will all be done baking at the same time. Make sure you fill your scoop well, without overfilling it.

· **Give 'em room.** Cookies need space to grow and spread, so space them 2 to 3 inches apart on your baking sheets. I mean it! Use an additional baking sheet if you need more surface area.

· **Is it done?** Are you trying to guess if your treats are done yet? Ask a grown-up to help find the light on your oven—then you can always watch through the glass! For most cookies, you will know it's time to take them out of the oven when the edges are slightly browning; but for chocolate cookies, it's best to rely on your timer.

· **Cool off.** The cookies in this book were designed to be eaten after they've cooled on their baking sheets. This means they may be a little soft (not to mention hot!) when you take them out of the oven, because they will continue to bake for a few minutes more on the hot baking sheet.

WHITE CHOCOLATE BLONDIES

FYI
Want thicker (but fewer) blondies? Bake these in an 8-inch square pan at 325°F for 30 to 35 minutes.

Makes 24 squares

In the world of desserts, brownies get all the attention. Yes, fudgy brownies do rule, but I think they have hogged the spotlight long enough. While we have been oohing and aahing over gooey dark chocolate squares, their white chocolate BFFs have been waiting for their time to shine. As the snow falls and you work up an appetite building that epic snowman in the yard, it's time you give the blondie a shot.

INGREDIENTS

1¾ cups flour

2 teaspoons kosher salt

½ teaspoon baking powder

1¼ cups + ⅔ cup white chocolate chips

3 sticks (24 tablespoons) unsalted butter

2 eggs

1 cup sugar

2 teaspoons vanilla extract

EQUIPMENT

OVEN

9 BY 13-INCH BAKING PAN

BAKING SPRAY

MIXING BOWLS

MEASURING CUPS + SPOONS

MICROWAVE + MICROWAVE-SAFE BOWL

RUBBER SPATULA

WHISK

TOOTHPICK

OVEN MITTS

FRIDGE OR FREEZER (OPTIONAL)

BUTTER KNIFE

PREP!

Preheat the oven to 325°F and coat the baking pan with baking spray.

MIX THE DRY!

In a medium bowl, combine the flour, salt, and baking powder.

MELT!

Combine the 1¼ cups white chocolate chips and the butter in a microwave-safe bowl and gently melt them in the microwave on medium power, in 30-second increments, stirring with a spatula between blasts. Once they are melted, whisk the mixture until smooth.

WHISK THE WET AND COMBINE!

In a large bowl, whisk the eggs, sugar, and vanilla together until smooth. Whisk in the white chocolate mixture. Whisk the dry ingredients into the wet mixture until smooth.

POUR AND BAKE!

Pour the batter into the prepared baking pan and sprinkle the remaining ⅔ cup white chocolate chips over the top. Bake at 325°F for 25 to 30 minutes, until golden brown and crispy around the edges, and a toothpick comes out clean when poked into the center (see page 23). Using oven mitts, remove the baking pan from the oven, and let the blondies cool completely in the pan. (I like to pop my pan in the fridge or freezer to speed this up.) Cut the blondie rectangle into 4 lengthwise rows and 6 crosswise rows, for a total of 24 squares. Store the blondies in an airtight container on the counter for up to 5 days or in the fridge for up to 2 weeks.

ROCKY ROAD CEREAL SQUARES

Makes 15 squares

If I had it my way, rocky road ice cream would be something I could put in my pocket and pull out whenever the craving strikes for something chocolaty, nutty, and gooey. Unfortunately, science has not created a non-meltable ice cream YET, and carrying a freezer around with me all day gets a little exhausting. My solution: Smoosh that chocolaty, nutty, marshmallowy goodness into some cereal and take that rocky road on the road!

FYI
The marshmallows will balloon up in a hilarious way when you microwave them, so make sure you use an oversize bowl.

INGREDIENTS

1 cup chocolate chips

1 cup plus 1 (10.5-ounce) bag mini marshmallows

5 tablespoons unsalted butter (save the paper it's wrapped in!)

½ cup almond butter

1 cup sliced almonds

8 cups Cocoa Rice Krispies cereal

EQUIPMENT

9 BY 13-INCH BAKING PAN

BAKING SPRAY

MEASURING CUPS + SPOONS

MICROWAVE + LARGE MICROWAVE-
  SAFE BOWL

RUBBER SPATULA

BUTTER KNIFE

PREP!

Coat the baking pan with baking spray. Sprinkle the chocolate chips and 1 cup of the mini marshmallows into the bottom of the prepared pan, spreading to make an even layer.

MELT!

In a very large microwave-safe bowl, melt the butter and the remaining mini marshmallows together for 2 minutes. Remove from the microwave and stir, then microwave for 1 more minute. Stir until smooth.

ADD MIX-INS!

Stir the almond butter into the melted marshmallows until well combined, then mix in the sliced almonds.

CEREAL TIME!

Add the Rice Krispies to the marshmallow mixture and stir with a spatula until every bit is coated.

SPREAD AND COOL!

Scrape the mixture into the baking pan and spread evenly with a greased spatula or with the butter paper (my grandma taught me this!). Let cool until firm, 15 to 20 minutes, then cut into 3 lengthwise and 5 crosswise rows to make a total of 15 squares. Store in an airtight container on your counter for up to 5 days.

FYI
Swap the cereal for whatever you love most (or whatever you've got in the cupboard)!

BANANA CRUNCH BREAD

Makes one loaf, 12 slices

This banana loaf is basically a zombie movie, but way, way less scary. Just when you thought those nearly black, weeks-old bananas on the counter were done for . . . BOOM, they are back and stronger than ever in the form of a crunch-topped, cakey treat. What's the only way to get rid of a zombie banana bread? Slice it, slather the slices with peanut butter-butter, and demolish it!

INGREDIENTS

1½ cups flour

1¼ teaspoons baking powder

1¼ teaspoons baking soda

1¼ teaspoons kosher salt

1½ cups mashed very rrrrripe bananas (about 3 medium bananas)

⅓ cup sour cream

1 cup sugar

1 stick (8 tablespoons) unsalted butter, melted

3 eggs

THE CRUNCH

¼ cup flour

¼ cup old-fashioned rolled oats

¼ cup light brown sugar

½ teaspoon kosher salt

2 tablespoons unsalted butter, melted

SERVING

Peanut butter-butter (recipe follows)

PREP!

Preheat the oven to 350°F and coat your loaf pan with baking spray.

MIX THE DRY!

In a medium bowl, combine the flour, baking powder, baking soda, and salt.

WHISK THE WET AND COMBINE!

In a large bowl, whisk together the banana, sour cream, and 1 cup sugar until well combined. Add the 8 tablespoons melted butter and whisk, then whisk in the eggs.

Then whisk the dry mixture into the banana mixture until well combined.

EQUIPMENT
FREEZER (OPTIONAL)
MICROWAVE (OPTIONAL)
OVEN
9 BY 5-INCH LOAF PAN
BAKING SPRAY
MIXING BOWLS
MEASURING CUPS + SPOONS
WHISK
RUBBER SPATULA OR WOODEN SPOON
TOOTHPICK
OVEN MITTS
BUTTER KNIFE

CRUNCH TIME!

In another medium bowl, combine all the crunch ingredients: the ¼ cup flour, the oats, brown sugar, salt, and butter, tossing until a small, rocky mixture forms.

POUR AND BAKE!

Pour the batter into your prepared loaf pan and smooth the top with the spatula or spoon. Sprinkle the crunch mix across the top in an even layer. Bake at 350°F for 55 to 60 minutes, until a toothpick comes out clean when poked into the center (see page 23). Using oven mitts, remove the loaf pan from the oven and let the loaf cool completely in the pan. Slice and serve with a dollop of the peanut butter-butter. Store on the counter in an airtight container for up to 1 week.

(recipe continues)

PEANUT BUTTER-BUTTER

Makes ½ cup

INGREDIENTS

1 stick (8 tablespoons) unsalted butter, softened

2 tablespoons peanut butter

EQUIPMENT

STAND MIXER WITH PADDLE ATTACHMENT

WHIP!

In the bowl of the mixer, combine the butter and peanut butter. Whip on medium speed for 2 minutes, until combined and fluffy. Serve at room temperature or store in the fridge for up to 1 week.

FYI

I make this loaf a lot, so I have developed a foolproof way to ensure I have rrrrripe bananas at all times: I buy just-ripe bananas and throw them, peel on, in an airtight container in the freezer to age for 2 days or up to 2 weeks. When ready to use, I defrost them in the microwave and remove the peels.

RRRRRIPE BANANAS

Bananas are masters of disguise. When you pick the up at the store, the peels m be a little green, indicating they're not quite ripe—whi is fine, as you've got time, c so you think! Nine times ou of ten, you place the banan in your fruit basket with ho and dreams of coming back to them for a tasty snack, only to find that magically overnight the bananas have gotten completely spotted and browned. But wait—th brown-spotted bananas ha lot of life in them still! Rrrr bananas (see the top banan pictured here) are perfect f Banana Crunch Bread, so d toss them.

If your bananas look mo like the middle banana, and you are itching to bake, I go you, too: See Monkey in the Middle Muffins (page 74) or Chunky Monkey Smoothies (page 75).

If you're living the botto banana life, wait a day or tw before using.

POT O' GOLD SHAKES

Makes 2 shakes

In the Milkshake Hall of Fame (™) you will find the best and most beloved shakes of all time: vanilla, chocolate, and strawberry, but king among them all is the Shamrock Shake. This is not a recipe for a Shamrock Shake, as that cannot be truly made at home and is only available in March. Instead, I suggest you get to know the Shamrock Shake's whimsical cousin, the Pot o' Gold Shake, leprechauns not included.

INGREDIENTS

4 large scoops of vanilla ice cream

½ cup milk

½ cup Lucky Charms cereal plus a few marshmallows

COMBINE AND BLEND!

Combine the ice cream, milk, and cereal in a blender and blend for 45 seconds, or until you reach your preferred thickness.

DRINK UP!

Pour into glasses, top with a few marshmallows, and have a blast.

LUCKY OBJECTS

Dice!

Rabbit foot!

Horseshoes!

Four-leaf clover!

EQUIPMENT

ICE CREAM/COOKIE SCOOP

MEASURING CUP

BLENDER

2 TALL GLASSES

Ladybugs!

Pennies on the ground!

REALLY GOOD FLAPJACKS

Makes 6 to 8 pancakes

My home away from home is a classic diner: hash browns that are griddled to perfection, stools that you can spin around on, and coffee that is terrible and amazing at the same time—you'll understand someday, promise. Whether I am dining with a crew (or, honestly, even solo) on a Sunday, I love to order a special "pancakes for the table." When everyone else is done ordering omelets and skillets, I ask for an extra stack of pancakes for us all to share. Ten times out of ten that stack of pancakes is destroyed by the end of breakfast—which proves a very important point: Everyone loves a really good pancake.

INGREDIENTS

1 cup flour

2 tablespoons sugar

1 tablespoon + 1 teaspoon baking powder

1 teaspoon kosher salt

¾ cup milk

1 egg

3 tablespoons vegetable oil

SERVING

Unsalted butter

Maple syrup

EQUIPMENT

MIXING BOWLS

MEASURING CUPS + SPOONS

WHISK

NONSTICK PAN OR GRIDDLE

BAKING SPRAY

PLASTIC SPATULA

WHISK THE DRY!

In a medium bowl, whisk together the flour, sugar, baking powder, and salt.

WHISK THE WET AND COMBINE!

In a small bowl, whisk together the milk, egg, and oil. Pour this into the flour mixture and whisk until your pancake batter is smooth.

COOK!

Coat a nonstick pan or griddle with baking spray and warm over medium heat. Pour ¼ cup of the batter into the prepared pan or griddle. Cook until the batter has set on the bottom and browned (bubbles will begin to appear on the top and a few will burst), 1 to 2 minutes. Flip carefully with a spatula and cook the other side until golden brown, 1 to 2 minutes more. Remove the pancake from the pan or griddle with the spatula. Repeat for the remaining batter, spraying again before cooking each one.

SERVE!

Serve the pancakes warm with a dollop of butter and a drizzle of maple syrup.

CITRUS SURPRISE CEREAL SQUARES

Makes 15 squares

Listen, I'm not normally a huge fan of surprises, at least not for receiving them! But when I bite into these zesty, chewy treats and find tiny green pebbles of pistachio, I am definitely not mad. It's a perfect BFF for the first days of spring, like when the snow is melting and pockets of green are starting to show themselves here and there, just when you were least expecting them. Fine, I guess surprises aren't that bad.

BTW
The marshmallows will balloon up in a hilarious way when you microwave them, so make sure you use an oversize bowl.

INGREDIENTS

5 tablespoons unsalted butter (save the paper it's wrapped in!)

1 (10.5-ounce) bag marshmallows

1 cup shelled pistachios, chopped

½ teaspoon lemon extract

7 cups Rice Krispies cereal

Swap the cereal for whatever you love most (or whatever you've got in the cupboard)! Ditto on the pistachios— use walnuts, or pecans, or almonds! You get the gist.

PREP!

Coat the baking pan with baking spray.

MELT!

In a very large, microwave-safe bowl, melt the butter and marshmallows together for 2 minutes. Remove from the microwave and stir, then microwave for 1 more minute. Stir until smooth.

ADD MIX-INS!

Stir the pistachios and lemon extract into the melted marshmallows.

CEREAL TIME!

Add the Rice Krispies to the marshmallow mixture, and stir with a spatula until every bit is coated.

SPREAD AND COOL!

Scrape the mixture into the prepared baking pan and spread evenly with a greased rubber spatula or with the butter paper (my grandma taught me this!). Let cool until firm, 15 to 20 minutes, then cut into 3 lengthwise rows and 5 crosswise rows to make 15 treats total. Store in an airtight container on your counter for up to 5 days.

FYI
Feel free to substitute the lemon extract with orange or grapefruit— any citrus flavor will do.

EQUIPMENT

9 BY 13-INCH BAKING PAN

BAKING SPRAY

MICROWAVE + LARGE MICROWAVE-
SAFE BOWL

RUBBER SPATULA

BUTTER KNIFE

BIRD BREAD

Makes one loaf, 12 slices

One of my favorite winter activities is to load up the bird feeder and watch as my winged friends swarm to feast. What is it about the seeds that drives these birds crazy? I had to find out more. I tried eating a handful of seeds on their own, but it turned into a big mess. (Don't actually eat birdseed.) Looking for a vehicle for seed consumption, I turned to birds' other fave food: bread. I baked the seeds into a loaf and realized: These birds are on to something! Now when I fill the feeder, I serve myself a slice of this loaf as a viewing snack.

INGREDIENTS

SEED MIX

½ cup old-fashioned rolled oats

3 tablespoons sesame seeds

3 tablespoons black sesame seeds

3 tablespoons poppy seeds

1 teaspoon kosher salt

BREAD

1½ sticks (12 tablespoons) unsalted butter, melted

½ cup light brown sugar

½ cup sugar

3 eggs

¼ cup vegetable oil

2 cups flour

1½ teaspoons baking powder

½ teaspoon baking soda

2 teaspoons kosher salt

1 teaspoon onion powder

PREP!

Preheat the oven to 350°F and coat the loaf pan with baking spray.

COMBINE THE SEED MIX!

In a small bowl, mix the oats, both sesame seeds, the poppy seeds, and salt. Set aside.

WHISK THE WET!

In a medium bowl, whisk the butter and both sugars together until well combined. Whisk in the eggs, then whisk in the oil.

MIX THE DRY AND COMBINE!

In another large bowl, combine the flour, baking powder, baking soda, salt, and onion powder. Add the butter mixture to the dry mixture, whisking until smooth. Set aside 2 tablespoons of the seed mixture, and stir the rest into the batter.

POUR AND BAKE!

Pour the batter into the prepared loaf pan and smooth the top with the spatula. Sprinkle the top with the remaining seed mixture. Bake at 350°F for 50 to 55 minutes, until a toothpick comes out clean when poked into the center (see page 23). Using oven mitts, remove the pan from the oven and let the bread cool completely in the pan. Slice and serve! Store on the counter in an airtight container for up to 1 week.

EQUIPMENT

OVEN

9 BY 5-INCH LOAF PAN

BAKING SPRAY

MIXING BOWLS

MEASURING CUPS + SPOONS

WHISK

RUBBER SPATULA OR WOODEN SPOON

TOOTHPICK

OVEN MITTS

BUTTER KNIFE

FYI
You want your butter to be soft and melty, not fully liquid and definitely not steaming hot. The best way to do this is in the microwave (in a microwave-safe bowl) on high for 30 seconds. If you need to heat it for longer (some microwaves are stronger than others), do it in 15-second bursts and take a look at it between zaps.

FYI
If you like a smaller (or larger) cookie, go for it—you're the boss, after all! Keep in mind that a smaller scoop will bake faster (reduce the bake time by 2 to 4 minutes) and a larger scoop will bake longer (increase the bake time by 2 to 4 minutes).

EARTH DAY COOKIES

Makes 18 to 24 cookies

FYI
The secret ingredient in these cookies is the milk powder; read up on it on page 19.

One of my secrets to life is celebrating *all* the holidays. When my calendar flips to April 22—aka Earth Day, which is a day to celebrate the big ball that we all call home, I make a big batch of these green and blue treats. Then I start planning my Arbor Day party (If you add a drop of green coloring to the blue dough, you'll make a brown dough; let your tree-loving imagination go wild!).

INGREDIENTS

2 cups flour

2 tablespoons nonfat milk powder

1¼ teaspoons kosher salt

½ teaspoon baking powder

¼ teaspoon baking soda

2 sticks (16 tablespoons) unsalted butter, super soft

¾ cup packed light brown sugar

½ cup sugar

1 egg

1 teaspoon vanilla extract

20 drops (¼ teaspoon) blue food coloring

10 drops green food coloring

EQUIPMENT

OVEN

2 BAKING SHEETS

BAKING SPRAY

MIXING BOWLS

RUBBER SPATULA

MEASURING CUPS + SPOONS

WOODEN SPOON

MICROWAVE + MICROWAVE-SAFE BOWL (OPTIONAL)

FRIDGE (OPTIONAL)

ICE CREAM/COOKIE SCOOP OR LARGE SPOON

OVEN MITTS

PREP!

Preheat the oven to 325°F. Coat the baking sheets with baking spray.

MIX THE DRY!

In a medium bowl, mix the flour, milk powder, salt, baking powder, and baking soda.

MIX THE WET AND COMBINE!

In a large bowl, and using a wooden spoon or sturdy rubber spatula, mix the butter and both sugars, flexing your muscles for about 2 minutes, until they are fully combined. Add the egg and vanilla, and stir until combined and fluffy, about 1 minute.

Add the dry mixture to the butter-sugar mixture, mixing until just combined. (If your dough is exceptionally wet—if it looks really shiny or oily—your butter was likely too hot. Throw it in the fridge for a few minutes to firm up before continuing on.)

ADD GREEN AND BLUE!

Divide your dough evenly between 2 bowls. In one bowl, add blue food coloring, and mix to combine. In the other bowl, add the green food coloring, and mix to combine. Add more drops as necessary to get the color you are looking for.

SCOOP AND SWIRL!

Scoop out a ball about 1 tablespoon in size from the blue dough and one from the green dough, then combine them with your hands and pinch the combined ball with your fingers to swirl the colors together slightly—so your ball looks like the earth! Roll into a smooth ball. Continue to make balls of the 2 colors until all the dough is used up.

BAKE!

Place the balls 2 to 3 inches apart on the prepared baking sheets. Bake the cookies at 325°F for 10 minutes. Double-check that you set the timer, because it's hard to tell by sight when they're ready to take out of the oven. The timer is your best friend! Using oven mitts, remove the baking sheets from the oven and cool the cookies completely on the baking sheets. Store in an airtight container for up to 1 week.

RISE AND SHINE CEREAL SQUARES

FYI
Swap the cereal for whatever you love most (or whatever you've got in the cupboard)!

Makes 15 squares

Some might say that breakfast is the most important meal of the day, but I am going to go on record to say that the midnight (8 P.M., if you've got a bedtime to get to) snack is pretty dang important, too. As I rush around the house in the morning, getting ready for the day's adventures, I don't always have time to sit down to a plate of eggs and toast. These treats have cereal *and* fruit *and* yogurt (technically!), so I am going to declare them a balanced breakfast as I grab one on my way out the door, or sneak one as my midnight snack.

INGREDIENTS

5 tablespoons unsalted butter (save the paper it's wrapped in!)

1 (10.5-ounce) bag marshmallows

1 cup yogurt-covered raisins

8 cups Cheerios cereal

PREP!

Coat the baking pan with baking spray.

MELT!

In a very large microwave-safe bowl, melt the butter and marshmallows together for 2 minutes. Remove from the microwave and stir, then microwave for 1 more minute. Stir until smooth.

ADD MIX-INS!

Stir the raisins into the marshmallow mixture.

CEREAL TIME!

Add the Cheerios to the marshmallow mixture and stir with a spatula until every bit is coated.

SPREAD AND COOL!

Scrape the mixture into the prepared baking pan and spread evenly with a greased spatula or with the butter paper (my grandma taught me this!). Let cool until firm, 15 to 20 minutes. Cut into 3 lengthwise rows and 5 crosswise rows, to make a total of 15 treats. Store in an airtight container on your counter for up to 5 days.

APRIL

EQUIPMENT

9 BY 13-INCH BAKING PAN

BAKING SPRAY

MICROWAVE + LARGE MIRCOWAVE-SAFE BOWL

RUBBER SPATULA

MEASURING CUPS + SPOONS

BUTTER KNIFE

FYI
The marshmallows will balloon up in a hilarious way when you microwave them, so make sure you use an oversize bowl.

CHEDDAR CHIVE BISCUITS

Makes 24 biscuits

If I could have breakfast with one "superhero," it would be the Easter Bunny. That's mostly because I have several questions for him/her/them—questions such as "How did ONE bunny get the gig of delivering baskets of candy to kids all over the world, and where do I apply for the job?" "Do you get to take the extra candy home with you?" "Why did you start this whole 'dyeing eggs' thing—I am into it, but I'm curious!" "Are your feet really lucky? If so, why?"

I would serve Dr. Bunny—the title is a professional courtesy—these cheesy, flaky, butter-packed, savory, green-flecked chive biscuits because I know Doc likes grass. I've seen the baskets!

INGREDIENTS

3 cups flour, plus extra for dusting

1 tablespoon baking powder

1 teaspoon baking soda

1 teaspoon kosher salt

1½ sticks (12 tablespoons) unsalted butter, cold, cut into ¼-inch cubes (yes, these are tiny, but you can do it!)

1¼ cups heavy cream

½ cup shredded cheddar cheese

2 tablespoons chopped chives or green onions

EQUIPMENT

BAKING SHEET

BAKING SPRAY

MIXING BOWLS

MEASURING CUPS + SPOONS

RULER

1½-INCH-WIDE ROUND COOKIE CUTTER

FRIDGE

OVEN

OVEN MITTS

PREP!

Coat the baking sheet with baking spray.

COMBINE AND MIX!

In a large bowl, combine the flour, baking powder, baking soda, and salt. Add the butter and pinch with your fingers, working until you no longer see chunks of butter, about 2 minutes. You will have a shaggy mixture.

STREAM THE CREAM!

Add the cream and mix gently with your hands to start. Once the cream is incorporated, pour in the cheese and chives, and start pressing and squeezing with your hands to bind the dough together.

ROLL AND CUT!

Dust a clean, dry section of your countertop with flour. Form your dough into a rectangle; the important part is that it ends up ½ inch thick (use a ruler!). Use the 1½-inch cookie cutter to cut out your biscuits. Smoosh together your leftover scraps, flatten again, and cut more biscuits, continuing this process until all the dough is used.

CHILL!

Place the biscuits on the prepared baking sheet and put in the refrigerator to chill for 30 minutes. Meanwhile, set your oven to 425°F.

BAKE!

Bake at 425°F for 12 minutes, or until the biscuits are golden brown at the edges. Using oven mitts, remove the baking sheet from the oven and let the biscuits cool on the sheet. These are best served warm, but you can also stash them in an airtight container for up to 3 days.

MONKEY IN THE MIDDLE MUFFINS

Makes 12 muffins

Everyone knows the best holiday is April Fools' Day. It's the one day when you are basically required to pull pranks on your friends and family. My favorite thing to do is mess with my family's food (in a delicious way, obviously)! On the outside these muffins appear super basic. I pretend they're just peanut butter–chocolate chip muffins; but when your unsuspecting target takes a bite, WHAM, banana town.

FYI
If you don't have buttermilk, you can DIY your own by combining ½ cup milk with ½ tablespoon lemon juice or white vinegar, and letting it sit on the counter for 10 minutes. Use immediately!

INGREDIENTS

2 cups flour

2 teaspoons baking powder

½ teaspoon baking soda

½ teaspoon kosher salt

1 egg

½ cup buttermilk

½ cup sugar

½ cup light brown sugar

1 teaspoon vanilla extract

1 cup vegetable oil

½ cup peanut butter, or any nut butter

½ cup chocolate chips

2 ripe medium bananas

EQUIPMENT

OVEN

12-CUP CUPCAKE/MUFFIN PAN

12 PAPER CUPCAKE LINERS

MIXING BOWLS

MEASURING CUPS + SPOONS

WHISK

RUBBER SPATULA

TOOTHPICK

OVEN MITTS

PREP!

Preheat the oven to 375°F. Line the cups of the muffin pan with the cupcake liners.

WHISK THE DRY!

In a large bowl, combine the flour, baking powder, baking soda, and salt.

WHISK THE WET!

In a medium bowl, whisk together the egg, buttermilk, both sugars, and the vanilla. Whisk in the oil and peanut butter until well combined.

Add the wet ingredients to the dry ingredients and whisk until smooth. Stir in the chocolate chips.

SCOOP!

Using a measuring cup, spoon ¼ cup of the batter into each cup of the muffin pan.

BANANA TIME!

Peel and slice each banana into 6 pieces. Place the banana pieces in the centers of the batter-filled muffin cups and push down to cover them with batter.

BAKE!

Bake the muffins at 375°F for 18 to 20 minutes, until the muffin tops brown slightly and a toothpick comes out clean when poked into the center of a muffin (see page 23). With oven mitts, take the muffin pan out of the oven. Let the muffins cool in the pan. These will last in an airtight container on your counter for 4 or 5 days.

APRIL

CHUNKY MONKEY SMOOTHIES

Makes 2 smoothies

I can't say for certain, but I have a pretty good hunch that monkeys like cereal. I mean, it's crunchy and sweet and comes in fun shapes and colors—all things that monkeys value. If you ever meet a monkey please, please get to the bottom of this theory and report back to me with your findings. In the meantime, here is a smoothie that the jungle dweller in all of us can appreciate. Plus, bananas bring potassium and the sense of humor we need this time of year, and always.

INGREDIENTS

1 banana, fresh or frozen

2 cups vanilla yogurt

2 cups cereal (such as Cinnamon Toast Crunch or Honey Nut Cheerios)

¼ cup honey

COMBINE AND BLEND!

Combine the banana, yogurt, cereal, and honey in a blender and blend for 45 seconds, or until you reach your preferred thickness.

DRINK UP!

Pour into glasses and have a blast.

FYI
If you have bananas that are going to the dark side, throw them in the freezer for Chunky Monkey time.

EQUIPMENT

FREEZER (OPTIONAL)

MEASURING CUPS

BLENDER

2 TALL GLASSES

monkey in the middle muffins,
page 74

ky monkey smoothies,
page 75

BLUEBERRY-LEMON PANCAKES

Makes 6 to 8 pancakes

If I'm being honest, I'm not a big fan of the term "brunch"—I'll keep my breakfast and lunch separate, thank you! What I do like are "breakfast parties"; after all, who said dinner should be the only meal that gets a celebration?! On sunny, spring mornings I whip up a few batches of these bright and fluffy blueberry pancakes, with some lemon glaze for the top. I crank up the tunes and invite my friends and fam over to hang. Best part: Pajamas and bedhead are required.

INGREDIENTS

1 cup flour

2 tablespoons sugar

1 tablespoon + 1 teaspoon baking powder

1 teaspoon kosher salt

¾ cup milk

1 egg

3 tablespoons vegetable oil

1 cup fresh or frozen blueberries

SERVING

1 batch (½ cup) lemon glaze (recipe follows)

EQUIPMENT

MIXING BOWLS

MEASURING CUPS + SPOONS

WHISK

NONSTICK PAN OR GRIDDLE

BAKING SPRAY

PLASTIC SPATULA

WHISK THE DRY!

In a medium bowl, whisk together the flour, sugar, baking powder, and salt.

WHISK THE WET AND COMBINE!

In a small bowl, whisk together the milk, egg, and oil. Pour this into the dry mixture and whisk until your pancake batter is mostly smooth. Stir in the blueberries.

COOK!

Coat your nonstick pan or griddle with baking spray and let it warm over medium heat. Pour ¼ cup batter into the prepared pan or onto the griddle. Cook until the batter has set on the bottom and browned (bubbles will begin to appear on the top and a few will burst), 1 to 2 minutes. Flip carefully with the spatula and cook the other side until golden brown, 1 to 2 minutes. Remove from the pan or griddle and keep warm. Repeat for the remaining pancakes.

SERVE!

Serve the pancakes warm and drizzled with the lemon glaze.

LEMON GLAZE

Makes ½ cup

INGREDIENTS

½ cup powdered sugar

1 tablespoon lemon juice

WHISK!

In a small bowl, whisk together the powdered sugar and lemon juice until smooth.

VEGGIE FRITTATA BITES

FYI
To bring these back to life on days 2, 3, 4, or 5, just zap 'em in the microwave for 15 seconds to make them as delicious as they were hot out of the oven.

Makes 12 muffins

Trying to make your mom extra proud on Mother's Day? (Every other day is cause for celebrating her, too. Take note.) A home-cooked breakfast is a strong move, but the real way to her heart is in showing her you heard her the gazillion times she told you to "eat your veggies." Frozen, fresh, leftover—the brilliant part of this recipe is that any veggie works, really. You're welcome for the bonus points. A handmade card and you are sure to win the #1 Kid award.

INGREDIENTS

12 eggs

¾ cup milk

2 teaspoons kosher salt

⅛ teaspoon ground black pepper

2 cups shredded cheese of your choosing

Veggies of choice (1½ cups if cooked, 2 cups if raw), cut into small pieces

PREP!

Preheat the oven to 400°F. Coat the cups of a muffin pan with baking spray.

WHISK!

In a large bowl, whisk together the eggs, milk, salt, and pepper until well combined.

LAYER!

Sprinkle 1 cup of the shredded cheese on the bottoms of the prepared cups in your muffin pan. Then, evenly spoon out your chopped veggies atop the cheese. Pour ¼ cup of your egg mixture into each veggie cup. Sprinkle the remaining 1 cup of cheese onto the egg batter in the cups.

BAKE!

Bake at 400°F for 20 minutes, until the tops of the muffins begin to brown slightly. With oven mitts, take the muffin pan out of the oven. Let the veggie bites cool slightly for 3 minutes, then carefully lift them out of the pan and serve them hot! These will last in an airtight container in your fridge for up to 5 days.

EQUIPMENT

OVEN

12-CUP CUPCAKE/MUFFIN PAN

BAKING SPRAY

LARGE MIXING BOWL

MEASURING CUPS + SPOONS

WHISK

RUBBER SPATULA

OVEN MITTS

MAY

DREAMSICLE BLONDIES

Makes 24 squares

My after-school sport of choice has always been track. The fresh air, the peace and quiet, the fun running shoes, the cool shorts—it is everything my competitive and adventure-seeking heart could want. Even better, race day meant all the orange slices I could eat. My mom was always there cheering me on, even when it embarrassed me and I begged her not to. When the pressure of a big race was making me tense and sweaty, Mom would have these citrusy, creamy bars waiting for me at the finish line, knowing I would run faster to get my hands on them!

FYI
Want thicker (but fewer) blondies? Bake these in an 8-inch square pan at 325°F for 30 to 35 minutes.

INGREDIENTS

1¼ cups white chocolate chips

3 sticks (24 tablespoons) unsalted butter

1¾ cups flour

2 teaspoons kosher salt

½ teaspoon baking powder

2 eggs

1 cup sugar

2 teaspoons vanilla extract

3 tablespoons Tang orange drink mix

6 tablespoons Marshmallow Fluff

EQUIPMENT

OVEN

9 BY 13-INCH BAKING PAN

BAKING SPRAY

MEASURING CUPS + SPOONS

MICROWAVE + MICROWAVE-SAFE BOWL

RUBBER SPATULA

WHISK

MIXING BOWLS

FORK

TOOTHPICK

OVEN MITTS

FRIDGE OR FREEZER (OPTIONAL)

BUTTER KNIFE

PREP!

Preheat the oven to 325°F and coat the baking pan with baking spray.

MELT!

Combine the white chocolate and butter in a microwave-safe bowl and gently melt them on medium power, in 30-second increments, stirring with a spatula between blasts. Once melted, whisk the mixture until smooth.

WHISK AND COMBINE!

In a medium bowl, combine the flour, salt, and baking powder. In a large bowl, whisk the eggs, sugar, and vanilla together until smooth. Whisk in the white chocolate mixture. Whisk your dry ingredients into your wet mixture until smooth.

POUR AND SWIRL!

Pour half the batter into the prepared baking pan. Stir the Tang powder into the remaining batter until it turns electric orange. Use a tablespoon to dollop the orange batter randomly onto the batter in the pan, then use another tablespoon to dollop on the marshmallow. With a fork, swirl the batters together, making sure to leave fun streaks of orange and white.

BAKE!

Bake at 325°F for 25 to 30 minutes, until golden brown and crispy around the edges, and a toothpick comes out clean when poked into the center (see page 23). Using oven mitts, remove the baking pan from the oven, and let the cake cool completely in the pan (I like to pop my pan in the fridge or freezer to speed this up). Cut into 4 lengthwise rows and 6 crosswise rows for a total of 24 squares. Store in an airtight container on the counter for up to 5 days or in the fridge for up to 2 weeks.

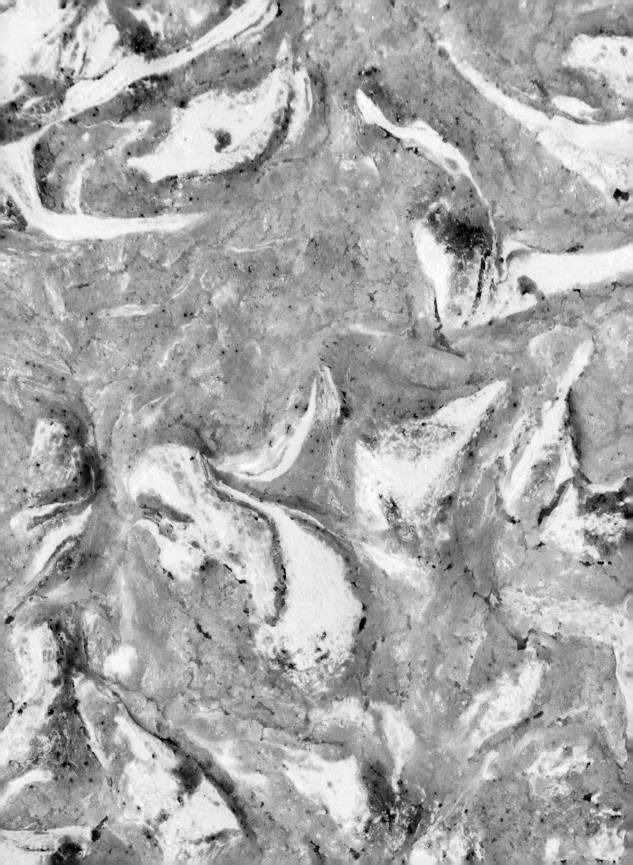

EASY AS PIE BARS

Makes 24 bar cookies

I was raised with a lot of rules: Brush your teeth every morning, make your bed, say please and thank you, be nice to your sister, and NEVER show up empty-handed. I may still be working on making my bed every morning, but I make it a point to never roll up to a party without something to contribute. These pie bars—like a slice of fruity pie with a crumble crust—come together quickly. They use five ingredients that I almost always have on hand, making them the perfect thing to whip up for a last-minute BBQ or picnic. Please and thank you!

FYI
If you're feeling crazy, add nuts (pecans, almonds, walnuts—whole or crushed) to the pie bottom or pie top. They add great flavor and texture!

INGREDIENTS

3⅔ cups flour

⅓ cup sugar

2 teaspoons kosher salt

2½ sticks (20 tablespoons) unsalted butter, melted

3 cups jam (two 12- or 13-ounce jars; we love raspberry, but whatever floats your boat!)

PREP!

Preheat the oven to 350°F and coat the baking pan with baking spray.

COMBINE AND PRESS!

In a large bowl stir together the flour, sugar, and salt. Add the melted butter, mixing until well combined. Using your hands, press 3 cups of the mixture into the bottom of your prepared baking pan, smooshing to make an even layer that fills to the corners. Keep the remaining mixture for the top.

SMOOTH AND SPRINKLE!

Using the back of a *metal* spoon, smooth the jam evenly on top of the crumb layer. Sprinkle (don't press) the remaining crumb mixture on top of the jam to make a loose, crumby top layer.

BAKE!

Bake at 350°F for 40 to 45 minutes, until the jam in the middle layer bubbles up and the crumb topping is golden brown (think the color of your favorite piecrust once baked!). Using oven mitts, remove the baking pan from the oven and let cool completely. Cut the cake into 4 lengthwise rows and 6 crosswise rows for a total of 24 squares. Store in an airtight container on the counter for up to 5 days or in the fridge for up to 2 weeks.

EQUIPMENT

OVEN

9 BY 13-INCH BAKING PAN

BAKING SPRAY

MIXING BOWL

MEASURING CUPS + SPOONS

WOODEN SPOON

METAL SPOON

OVEN MITTS

BUTTER KNIFE

LEFTOVER WAFFLE

Makes 1 waffle

You know the expression "one man's trash is another man's treasure"? Well, I like to say "one person's dinner is myyyy breakfast." If your parents are like mine, your fridge is overflowing with leftovers, begging to be given a second chance. I have news for you: If you can dream it, you can waffle it! Mashed potato waffles? Stuffing waffles? Chicken nugget waffles? Breakfast. Is. SERVED.

FYI
If your waffle is sweet, serve it with maple or chocolate syrup or jam. If your waffle is savory, serve it with a dollop of butter, mustard, or ketchup.

INGREDIENTS
1 cup of your favorite leftovers—mashed potatoes, mac 'n' cheese, stuffing, fried rice, and so on. Experiment! But soup is off limits.

SERVING
Dipping sauce or topping, your choice

PREP!
Turn on the waffle maker and set it to low heat.

SCOOP AND COOK!
Scoop your leftover of choice onto the waffle maker and use a spoon to spread it out to the edge. Close the waffle maker and cook for 10 minutes.

You need to cook your leftovers low and slow to get them crispy on the outside and soft on the inside—don't rush it!

SERVE!
Serve warm, with any dipping sauce or topping you see fit.

MAY

Will it waffle?!
Match the food to the answer!

COLUMN A	COLUMN B
Hash browns	Genius
Oatmeal	Yum
Soup	Into it
French toast	Perf!
Cookie dough	No way

EQUIPMENT
WAFFLE MAKER
SPOON

FYI
This extra-large cookie technique works *awesomely* with chocolate chip cookies (see page 135), butterscotch cookies (see page 192), or choco crunch cookies (see page 48).

MINT COOKIES AND CREAM COOKIE PIE

Makes one 8-inch large cookie, cut into 8 slices, pizza-style

It's the last day of school and you need to bring something BIG to celebrate the beginning of summer. Sure, cupcakes would work, and no one would be mad about a batch of regular cookies. But is that how you really want to celebrate this momentous occasion? You need to pull out your best moves. Two words, my friend: cookie. pie. This mall classic, peppered with the ultimate combo of mint and chocolate, is every bit as ridiculous and over the top as it is delicious and irresistible. I guarantee *everyone* will want to sign your yearbook after they have had a slice.

FYI
You want your butter to be soft and melty, not fully liquid and definitely not steaming hot. The best way to do this is in the microwave (in a microwave-safe bowl) on high for 30 seconds. If you need to heat it for longer (some microwaves are stronger than others), do it in 15-second bursts, and take a look at it between zaps.

INGREDIENTS

¾ cup flour

2 tablespoons cocoa powder

1 tablespoon nonfat milk powder

½ teaspoon kosher salt

¼ teaspoon baking powder

⅛ teaspoon baking soda

1 stick (8 tablespoons) unsalted butter, super soft

⅓ cup sugar

¼ cup light brown sugar

1 egg

1 teaspoon mint extract

½ teaspoon vanilla extract

¼ cup white chocolate chips, plus more for the top

2 tablespoons chocolate chips, plus more for the top

5 mint chocolate Oreos cookies, broken into pieces, plus more for the top

PREP!
Preheat the oven to 350°F. Coat the baking sheet and chosen baking pan with baking spray.

MIX THE DRY!
In a medium bowl, mix the flour, cocoa powder, milk powder, salt, baking powder, and baking soda.

MIX THE WET AND COMBINE!
In a large bowl, and using a wooden spoon or sturdy rubber spatula, mix the butter and both sugars, flexing your muscles for about 2 minutes, until they are fully combined. Add the egg, mint, and vanilla and stir until combined and fluffy, about 1 minute.

Add the dry mixture to the wet mixture, mixing until just combined. (If your dough is exceptionally wet—if it looks really shiny or oily—your butter was likely too hot. Throw it in the fridge for a few minutes to firm up before continuing.)

CHOCOLATE TIME!
Fold in the white chocolate chips, chocolate chips, and crushed cookies. (Save a few tablespoons of each for the next step, though.)

EQUIPMENT

OVEN

BAKING SHEET

8-INCH PIE PAN, 8-INCH ROUND CAKE RING, OR 8-INCH SPRINGFORM PAN

BAKING SPRAY

MIXING BOWLS

MEASURING CUPS + SPOONS

MICROWAVE + MIRCOWAVE-SAFE BOWL (OPTIONAL)

WOODEN SPOON OR RUBBER SPATULA

FRIDGE (OPTIONAL)

OVEN MITTS

(recipe continues)

MAY

SPREAD, SPRINKLE, AND BAKE!

Place the prepared baking pan on top of the baking sheet. Smoosh your dough into the bottom of the pan. Using your hands, pat the dough down evenly to the edges. Sprinkle some extra cookies and chocolate chips around the inside edge of your ring as decoration. Bake the cookie at 350°F for 18 to 20 minutes. Double-check that you set the timer; because this cookie is already dark brown it's tricky to tell by sight when it's ready to take out of the oven. The timer is your best friend! Using oven mitts, remove the baking sheet and pan from the oven and let the cookie cool completely on the baking sheet (about 25 minutes). Cut the cookie into 8 slices, like a pizza. Store the slices on a plate, wrapped well in plastic, for up to 1 week.

FYI
The secret ingredient in these cookies is the milk powder; read up on it on page 19.

MAY

CHOCOLATE COCONUT CUPCAKES

Makes 12 frosted cupcakes

Dear nine-year-old Christina,

I know you think you don't like chocolate and coconut. You see Mom eating her fancy dark chocolate candy bars, leaving crumbs of white flaky coconut behind, and in your head you say *Yuck! Grown-ups eat the grossest stuff!* I have some news from the future: The chocolate and coconut combo is pretty epic! It's deep and rich and zippy and fluffy all at the same time, and soon you won't be able to get enough of it. So stop wasting your time hatin' and give these cupcakes a try!

XO,

Undercover Grown-Up Christina

P.S. Please tell Mom to stop giving you and your sister bowl cuts. Trust me, it's not your look.

---

1 batch (12) coconut cupcakes (recipe follows)

1 batch (2 cups) dark chocolate frosting (recipe follows)

ASSEMBLE!

Dollop a large spoonful of dark chocolate frosting—about 2 tablespoons—on top of each cupcake. Use the back side of your spoon to smooth your frosting into an even and fluffy layer. Serve! Store in a large airtight container on the counter for up to 3 days or in the fridge for up to 1 week.

(recipe continues)

COCONUT CUPCAKES

Makes 12 cupcakes

INGREDIENTS

1¼ cups flour

1 tablespoon baking powder

¾ teaspoon kosher salt

½ stick (4 tablespoons) unsalted butter, melted

¾ cup sugar

3 tablespoons light brown sugar

2 eggs

½ cup vegetable oil

1 teaspoon vanilla extract

⅔ cup buttermilk

1 cup sweetened flaked coconut

PREP!

Preheat the oven to 350°F. Line the cups of the cupcake pan with the cupcake liners.

MIX THE DRY!

In a large bowl, combine the flour, baking powder, and salt.

WHISK THE WET AND COMBINE!

In a medium bowl, whisk together the butter, both sugars, and the eggs until well combined. Whisk in the oil and vanilla. Whisk in the buttermilk.

Then whisk the wet ingredients into the dry ingredients until smooth. Stir in the coconut.

SCOOP AND BAKE!

Use a ¼-cup measure to scoop portions of your batter into the cupcake cups. The batter will be almost level with the top edge of the liner (but it shouldn't go over!). Bake for 15 to 20 minutes at 350°F, until the tops brown slightly and a toothpick comes out clean when poked into the center of a cupcake (see page 23). Using oven mitts, remove the pan from the oven and let the cupcakes cool completely in the pan.

FYI
If you don't have buttermilk, you can DIY your own by combining ⅔ cup milk wit 2 teaspoons lemon juice o white vinegar, and letting it sit on the counter for 10 minutes. Use immediately!

EQUIPMENT

OVEN

12-CUP CUPCAKE/MUFFIN PAN

12 PAPER CUPCAKE LINERS

MIXING BOWLS

MEASURING CUPS + SPOONS

WHISK

RUBBER SPATULA

TOOTHPICK

OVEN MITTS

JUNE

DARK CHOCOLATE FROSTING

Makes 2 cups

INGREDIENTS

1½ sticks (12 tablespoons) unsalted butter, softened

2¼ cups powdered sugar

⅓ cup cocoa powder

3 tablespoons milk

¾ teaspoon vanilla extract

¼ teaspoon kosher salt

MIX!

Starting on low speed, use the mixer to combine your butter, powdered sugar, and cocoa powder, 1 minute. Increase the mixer speed to medium and whip until super smooth, about 3 minutes. Turn off the mixer. Use your spatula to scrape down the sides of your bowl well.

ADD AND FLUFF!

Add the milk, vanilla, and salt. Continue mixing until combined and fluffy, about 1 minute.

EQUIPMENT

HAND MIXER OR STAND MIXER WITH
   PADDLE ATTACHMENT

LARGE MIXING BOWL

MEASURING CUPS + SPOONS

RUBBER SPATULA

DINNER SPOON

GAZILLIONAIRE'S BARS

Makes 24 bar cookies

If I were a gazillionaire, I would give everyone a pair of Rollerblades, because traffic stinks and blading is the best way to travel. I'd lobby to make the bottom layer of the food pyramid be cookies, cakes, and ice cream. Trampolines would be mandatory in every gym. Pizza ATMs would replace boring cash machines. Each town would have a puppy library, where you could check out a dog friend for the day, free of charge. Everyone would get to go to the moon—at least once. And I would serve these wonderfully rich, chocolatey-sweet bars for breakfast, lunch, and dinner.

FYI
This recipe is very flexible—add any other fun pantry snacks for even more flavor, texture, and fun.

INGREDIENTS

2 cups crushed cookies (about 26 Oreos)

½ stick (4 tablespoons) unsalted butter, melted

1 cup cereal of choice (we love Cocoa Krispies)

½ cup chocolate chips

24 whole mini pretzels

1 (14-ounce) can sweetened condensed milk

EQUIPMENT

OVEN

9 BY 13-INCH BAKING PAN

BAKING SPRAY

MEASURING CUPS + SPOONS

MIXING BOWL

OVEN MITTS

FRIDGE OR FREEZER (OPTIONAL)

BUTTER KNIFE

PREP!

Preheat the oven to 350°F and coat the baking pan with baking spray.

LAYER UP!

Using your hands, combine the crushed cookies with the melted butter and press them into the bottom of your prepared baking pan, smooshing to make an even layer that fills all the way to the corners. Sprinkle the cereal evenly atop the cookie layer. Then sprinkle the chocolate chips evenly over the cereal layer. Finally, evenly place the 24 pretzels in a grid on top of your chocolate chip layer.

FYI
Want thicker (but fewer) squares? Bake this in an 8-inch square pan, at 325°F for 15 to 20 minutes instead.

POUR!

Pour the sweetened condensed milk straight from the can in a drizzling fashion over the entire baking pan, working quickly to get an even layer. This layer will ooze and smooth itself out in the oven; don't try to smooth it with a spatula, even if you're unhappy with your drizzle.

BAKE!

Bake at 350°F for 20 to 25 minutes, until the sweetened condensed milk is golden brown on top. Using oven mitts, remove the baking pan from the oven, and let the bars cool completely in the pan (I like to pop my pan in the fridge or freezer to speed this up). Cut the bars into 4 lengthwise rows and 6 crosswise rows, making a total of 24 bars. Store in an airtight container on the counter for up to 5 days or in the fridge for up to 2 weeks.

JUNE

RASPBERRY-LEMON RICOTTA TEA CAKE

Makes one loaf, 12 slices

I have never been one for tea parties, maybe because they usually feature imaginary food and that is just too much of a tease for me to handle. Where's all the tasty tea cake—for real?! I'd like to submit for formal consideration this berry-filled, citrusy loaf for every tea party here on out, as well as all other springtime celebrations, such as:

- Mothers' Day Breakfast
- First Picnic of the Year Sunday

- 4th Annual It's Finally Warm Enough to Not Wear a Jacket Day Party

- Random Tuesday Snack Time
- The Spring Cleaning Ball

INGREDIENTS

1¾ cups flour

1 teaspoon baking powder

1 teaspoon kosher salt

1¼ cups sugar

2 tablespoons light brown sugar

1 cup ricotta

3 eggs

1 stick (8 tablespoons) unsalted butter, melted

½ cup buttermilk

⅓ cup vegetable oil

1 tablespoon vanilla extract

2 teaspoons lemon extract

½ pint fresh raspberries

SERVING
Honey butter (recipe follows)

PREP!
Preheat the oven to 325°F and coat the loaf pan with baking spray.

MIX THE DRY!
In a medium bowl, combine the flour, baking powder, and salt.

MIX THE WET AND COMBINE!
In a large bowl, whisk together both sugars and the ricotta. Once combined, whisk in the eggs. In a medium bowl, combine the butter, buttermilk, oil, and vanilla and lemon extracts. Then whisk this combo into the ricotta and sugar mixture.

Add the dry mixture to the wet and whisk until smooth.

BERRY TIME!
Once you have a smooth batter, take out 8 good-looking raspberries and set them aside. Gently stir the rest of the raspberries into the batter.

POUR AND BAKE!
Pour the batter into your prepared loaf pan, smooth the batter with your wooden spoon, and decorate the top with your remaining raspberries. Bake at 325°F for 60 to 65 minutes, until a toothpick comes out clean when poked into the center of the loaf (see page 23). Using oven mitts, remove the loaf pan from the oven and let the cake cool completely in the pan. Slice and serve with a dollop of the honey butter. Store on the counter in an airtight container for up to 1 week.

EQUIPMENT
OVEN

9 BY 5-INCH LOAF PAN

BAKING SPRAY

MIXING BOWLS

MEASURING CUPS + SPOONS

WHISK

WOODEN SPOON

TOOTHPICK

OVEN MITTS

BUTTER KNIFE

JUNE

HONEY BUTTER

Makes ½ cup

INGREDIENTS

**1 stick (8 tablespoons)
unsalted butter, softened**

2 tablespoons honey

WHIP!

In the bowl of the stand mixer, combine your butter and honey. Whip on medium speed for 2 minutes, until combined and fluffy. Transfer into a serving bowl, scraping the sides of the mixer bowl well. Serve at room temperature.

EQUIPMENT

STAND MIXER WITH PADDLE ATTACHMENT

MEASURING SPOON

RUBBER SPATULA

SERVING BOWL

BUTTER KNIFE

JUNE

GRANOLA COOKIES

Makes 12 to 18 cookies

My grandma made the greatest version of these cookies—and we all know that when it comes to cookies, #GrandmaKnowsBest. These are basically the chewiest oatmeal cookies around, and one of my all-time faves. She always had dough in the fridge ready to be baked at a moment's notice. When she heard our car pull in, she'd crouch down like a linebacker in front of the oven because when the timer went off, I'd come running fast, and she'd have to defend the batch with all she had.

FYI
If you like a smaller (or larger) cookie, go for it—you're the boss, after all! Keep in mind that a smaller cookie will bake faster (reduce the bake time by 2 to 4 minutes) and a larger one will need to bake longer (increase the bake time by 2 to 4 minutes).

INGREDIENTS

1⅔ cups flour

2¼ cups granola

½ cup sweetened shredded coconut

1¼ teaspoons ground cinnamon

1¼ teaspoons kosher salt

1 teaspoon baking soda

2 sticks (16 tablespoons) unsalted butter, super soft

¾ cup packed light brown sugar

⅔ cup sugar

2 eggs

2 teaspoons vanilla extract

1 cup powdered sugar

EQUIPMENT

OVEN

2 BAKING SHEETS

BAKING SPRAY

MIXING BOWLS

MEASURING CUPS + SPOONS

WOODEN SPOON OR FIRM RUBBER SPATULA

MICROWAVE + MICROWAVE-SAFE BOWL (OPTIONAL)

ICE CREAM/COOKIE SCOOP

OVEN MITTS

PREP!
Preheat the oven to 350°F. Coat the baking sheets with baking spray.

MIX THE DRY!
In a medium bowl, mix the flour, granola, coconut, cinnamon, salt, and baking soda.

MIX THE WET!
In a large bowl, and using a wooden spoon or spatula, mix the butter and both sugars, flexing your muscles for about 2 minutes, until they are fully combined. Add the eggs and vanilla and stir until combined and fluffy, about 1 minute.

Add the dry mixture to the wet mixture, mixing until just combined. (If you have made some of the other cookies in this book and think this dough looks a bit wetter than the others, don't worry, you are doing it right!)

SCOOP AND ROLL!
Put the powdered sugar into a small bowl. Scoop the dough into balls about 2 tablespoons in size and roll them between your hands until they are smooth. Toss the balls of dough individually into the powdered sugar until they are completely covered, then place them on the prepared baking sheets, 2 to 3 inches apart.

BAKE!
Bake the cookies at 350°F for 10 to 12 minutes, until golden brown. Using oven mitts, remove the baking sheets from the oven and cool the cookies completely on the baking sheets. Store in an airtight container for a week.

BTW
If you're not into coconut, feel free to omit it!

NUT-N-JAMMIE COOKIE SAMMIES

Makes 12 cookie sandwiches

In my book, if you slather jam on something, that makes it a breakfast item. Listen, I don't make the food rules, I just obey them, especially when it means I can justify eating two cookies with some jam wedged between them while I watch my morning cartoons. This nut-and-fruit combo does work great in the A.M., but don't snooze on the breakfast-for-dinner concept, either—these sammies make a great P.M. treat as well!

1½ cups jam, you choose the flavor!

1 batch (24) cut-out sandies (recipe follows)

STACK!
Swirl a dollop of jam (about 2 tablespoons) on the bottom of one of the cut-out cookies, smoothing with the back of a spoon to make an even layer. Top the jam with the bottom of another cut-out cookie (so jam is between the bottom surfaces and the outsides are the cookie tops) and press together, squeezing just until the jam oozes to the edge of the cookie. Repeat with the remaining cookies. Pop in the fridge for 15 minutes to let the jam firm up before serving. Store in an airtight container on the counter for up to 1 week or in the freezer for up to 1 month—they're pretty awesome frozen!

CUT-OUT SANDIES

Makes 24 cookies

FYI
Chilling the dough makes it easier to roll out, *plus* you can easily stash one bag of dough for later.

INGREDIENTS

2 sticks (16 tablespoons) unsalted butter, softened

½ cup packed light brown sugar

1 teaspoon vanilla extract

2 cups flour, plus more for dusting

½ teaspoon kosher salt

½ cup finely crushed nuts of your choosing

EQUIPMENT

2 BAKING SHEETS

BAKING SPRAY

MIXING BOWL

MEASURING CUPS + SPOONS

WOODEN SPOON OR STAND MIXER WITH PADDLE ATTACHMENT

3 ZIP-TOP PLASTIC BAGS OR PLASTIC WRAP

FRIDGE

OVEN

ROLLING PIN

RULER

2-INCH ROUND COOKIE CUTTER

PLASTIC SPATULA

OVEN MITS

PREP!

Coat the baking sheets with baking spray.

COMBINE!

In a large bowl, combine the butter, brown sugar, and vanilla using a wooden spoon (or stand mixer). Mix until the butter and brown sugar are smooth, about 2 minutes by hand (or 45 seconds in the mixer). Add the flour, salt, and nuts and stir or mix until well combined (if you're not using a mixer, it may be easiest to ditch the spoon and use your hands to form the dough).

SHAPE AND CHILL!

Form the dough into a ball, and divide the ball into 3 pieces. Place each piece in a plastic bag and pat the dough smooth and flat with your hands. Refrigerate the bags of dough for 15 minutes. Meanwhile, preheat the oven to 350°F.

FYI
If you have leftover scraps of dough after you have cut out your cookies, combine them into a ball and roll it out anew to cut out more cookies. If the dough gets too sticky, chill it in the fridge for 15 minutes.

ROLL AND CUT!

Dust a clean, dry section of your countertop with a little flour. Take a piece of dough out of the plastic bag and place on the counter. Dust the rolling pin with a little flour and roll out the dough until it is ¼ inch thick (use a ruler!). Use the 2-inch cookie cutter to cut your dough into rounds. (If you want, you can cut a small hole out of half the cookies—the top ones—to show the filling.) Using a spatula, lift the rounds and transfer them to your prepared baking sheets. Repeat with the remaining 2 packages of dough.

BAKE!

Bake the cookies at 350°F for 13 to 15 minutes, until the edges of the cookies are golden brown. With oven mitts, remove the baking sheets from the oven and cool the cookies completely on the baking sheets.

WATERMELON LIME SMOOTHIES

Makes 2 smoothies

Fact: A cold watermelon slush on a hot summer day is one of the greatest joys in life. Blend this up, snag a pair of sunglasses—the more outrageous the better—and embrace the heat.

INGREDIENTS

4 cups cubed seedless watermelon

2 teaspoons lime juice

1 cup ice cubes

EQUIPMENT

MEASURING CUPS + SPOONS
BLENDER
2 TALL GLASSES

COMBINE AND BLEND!

Combine the watermelon, lime juice, and ice cubes in a blender and blend for 45 seconds, or until you reach your preferred thickness.

DRINK UP!

Pour into glasses and serve ASAP for maximum coolness.

SUMMER WORD SEARCH!

Grab a pencil and your shades and look for these words while you slurp!

BIKE

JUMP

LIME

SPLASH

SPRINKLER

SUN

S	O	P	R	T	R	X	Z	H	Z	N	Q	X	J	P
T	P	U	P	T	B	S	C	M	R	B	A	Z	K	K
T	E	R	B	S	D	B	L	X	T	Y	W	I	O	P
X	Q	O	I	E	M	I	L	X	G	C	E	K	Y	T
E	S	Q	W	N	H	R	Z	M	U	O	Q	R	V	Z
A	P	Z	A	G	K	Z	D	O	V	X	R	D	S	O
Y	L	B	C	H	G	L	B	Q	A	U	K	W	P	M
H	A	I	P	F	Z	I	E	Y	F	G	Z	S	V	V
A	S	Q	H	M	K	X	A	R	J	E	N	P	N	T
X	H	N	A	E	U	M	C	H	Y	D	B	W	U	B
E	U	H	F	U	D	J	C	N	Z	E	E	B	S	I
T	Y	L	I	N	O	A	P	A	O	A	Z	Z	P	D
Z	D	T	F	P	Z	M	J	C	Y	Q	E	H	U	X
E	C	G	D	S	A	Z	O	X	I	O	K	X	D	A
R	K	W	K	H	M	X	Q	L	M	T	V	B	K	Z

JUNE

TROPICAL MERMAID MUFFINS

Makes 12 muffins

In my house, when summer finally comes we crave water and swimsuits! Wading, swimming, or running through the water always makes me dream of being a mermaid. I feel this way whether the water is from a sprinkler, a blow-up pool, the river, ocean—or heck, even a bathtub does the job. These pineapple-coconut creations are the key to living out your mermaid daydreams, so complete the scene with your flashiest beach towel. Splish, splash!

FYI
If you don't have buttermilk, you can DIY your own by combining ½ cup milk with ½ tablespoon lemon juice or white vinegar, and letting it sit on the counter for 10 minutes. Use immediately!

INGREDIENTS

2 cups flour

2 teaspoons baking powder

½ teaspoon baking soda

¼ teaspoon kosher salt

1 egg

¾ cup sugar

½ cup buttermilk

1 teaspoon vanilla extract

¾ cup vegetable oil

¾ cup canned crushed pineapple, drained

½ cup sweetened coconut flakes

PREP!

Preheat the oven to 375°F. Line the cups of a muffin pan with the cupcake liners.

MIX THE DRY!

In a large bowl, combine the flour, baking powder, baking soda, and salt.

In a medium bowl, whisk together the egg, sugar, buttermilk, and vanilla. Whisk in the oil.

Add the wet ingredients to the dry ingredients and whisk until smooth. Stir in the pineapple and coconut.

SCOOP AND BAKE!

Using a measuring cup, spoon ⅓ cup of the batter into each muffin cup. The batter will reach right up under the lip of the cupcake liner (but shouldn't go over!). Bake at 375°F for 18 to 20 minutes, until the muffin tops brown slightly and a toothpick comes out clean when poked into the center of a muffin (see page 23). With oven mitts, take the muffin pan out of the oven. Let the muffins cool in the pan. These will last in an airtight container on your counter for 4 or 5 days.

EQUIPMENT

OVEN

12-CUP CUPCAKE/MUFFIN PAN

12 PAPER CUPCAKE LINERS

MIXING BOWLS

MEASURING CUPS + SPOONS

WHISK

RUBBER SPATULA

TOOTHPICK

OVEN MITTS

STRAWBERRIES AND CREAM CUPCAKES

Makes 12 frosted cupcakes

In my eyes, there are five different times of year: fall, winter, spring, summer—and (the best of all), Berry Season. When berries are at their peak, usually toward the end of July where I live but maybe earlier or later for you, I cannot get enough of them. If I get tired of eating strawberries by the handful or blending them into my morning smoothie (see page 121), my next play is to make them into a frosting for my favorite vanilla cupcakes.

1 batch (12) vanilla cupcakes (recipe follows)

1 batch (2 cups) strawberry frosting (recipe follows)

ASSEMBLE!

Dollop a large spoonful of strawberry frosting (about 2 tablespoons) on top of each cupcake. Use the back side of your spoon to smooth the frosting into an even and fluffy layer. Serve the same day as you frost the cupcakes!

(recipe continues)

VANILLA CUPCAKES

Makes 12 cupcakes

INGREDIENTS

1¾ cups flour

1 tablespoon baking powder

½ teaspoon kosher salt

½ stick (4 tablespoons) unsalted butter, melted

¾ cup sugar

2 tablespoons light brown sugar

2 eggs

½ cup vegetable oil

2 teaspoons vanilla extract

½ cup buttermilk

PREP!

Preheat the oven to 350°F. Line the cups of the cupcake pan with the cupcake liners.

MIX THE DRY!

In a large bowl, combine your flour, baking powder, and salt.

WHISK THE WET!

In a medium bowl, whisk together your butter, sugars, and eggs until well combined. Whisk in the oil and vanilla. Whisk in the buttermilk.

Then whisk your wet ingredients into the dry ingredients until smooth.

SCOOP AND BAKE!

Use a ¼-cup measure to scoop portions of your batter into the lined cups of the cupcake pan. The batter will be almost level with the top edge of the cup (but it shouldn't go over!). Bake at 350°F for 15 to 20 minutes, until the tops of the cupcakes brown slightly and a toothpick comes out clean when poked into the center of a cupcake (see page 23). Using oven mitts, remove the cupcake pan from the oven and cool the cupcakes completely in the pan.

FYI
If you don't have buttermilk, you can DIY your own by combining ½ cup milk with ½ tablespoon lemon juice or white vinegar, and letting it sit on the counter for 10 minutes. Use immediately!

EQUIPMENT

OVEN

12-CUP CUPCAKE/MUFFIN PAN

12 PAPER CUPCAKE LINERS

MIXING BOWLS

MEASURING CUPS + SPOONS

WHISK

RUBBER SPATULA

TOOTHPICK

OVEN MITTS

STRAWBERRY FROSTING

Makes 2 cups

INGREDIENTS

¾ cup fresh strawberries (5 or 6 berries, depending on size)

1½ sticks (12 tablespoons) unsalted butter, softened

1½ cups powdered sugar

¼ teaspoon kosher salt

PREP!

Cut off the leafy tops of the strawberries with a butter knife, then slice the strawberries.

MIX!

Starting on a low speed, use a mixer to combine your butter and powdered sugar, 1 minute. Increase the mixer speed to medium and whip until super smooth, about 3 minutes. Turn off the mixer. Use your spatula to scrape down the sides of your bowl well.

ADD AND FLUFF!

Add the strawberries and salt. Continue mixing until combined and fluffy, about 1 minute.

FYI
This frosting is *out of this world*. The only thing is, you have to use it soon after you make it and then serve the cupcakes the same day; otherwise the strawberries get soggy and lose flavor!

EQUIPMENT

BUTTER KNIFE

CUTTING BOARD

HAND MIXER OR STAND MIXER WITH PADDLE ATTACHMENT

MIXING BOWL

MEASURING CUPS + SPOONS

RUBBER SPATULA

DINNER SPOON

CHOCOLATE MUFFINS

Makes 12 muffins

If you think that I created this muffin solely so I could eat chocolate for breakfast . . . you may be right. But the good news is that now you can eat chocolate for breakfast, too! These muffins really shine on the days when the fridge is empty and you have nothing extra around the kitchen, or when a plain, old gray day isn't filling you with inspiration. Serve these with a cold glass of chocolate milk if you are really getting after it. And don't forget sometimes you need chocolate muffins for other times of the year, too.

INGREDIENTS

2 cups flour

¼ cup cocoa powder

1 tablespoon baking powder

½ teaspoon baking soda

½ teaspoon kosher salt

2 eggs

1½ cups sugar

1 cup buttermilk

1 teaspoon vanilla extract

1 cup vegetable oil

1 cup chocolate chips

PREP!

Preheat the oven to 375°F. Line the cups of the muffin pan with the cupcake liners.

MIX THE DRY!

In a large bowl, combine the flour, cocoa powder, baking powder, baking soda, and salt.

WHISK THE WET!

In a medium bowl, whisk together the eggs, sugar, buttermilk, and vanilla. Whisk in the oil.

Add the wet ingredients to the dry ingredients and whisk until smooth. Stir in the chocolate chips.

SCOOP AND BAKE!

Using a measuring cup, spoon ⅓ cup of the batter into each muffin cup in the pan. The batter will reach right under the lip of the cupcake liner (but shouldn't go over!). Bake at 375°F for 20 to 22 minutes, until a toothpick comes out clean when poked into the center of a muffin (see page 23). Double-check that you set the timer; because these muffins are already dark brown, it's impossible to tell by sight when they're ready to take out of the oven. The timer is your best friend! With oven mitts, take the muffin pan out of the oven. Let the muffins cool in the pan. These will last in an airtight container on your counter for 4 or 5 days.

EQUIPMENT

OVEN

12-CUP CUPCAKE/MUFFIN PAN

12 PAPER CUPCAKE LINERS

MIXING BOWLS

MEASURING CUPS + SPOONS

WHISK

RUBBER SPATULA

TOOTHPICK

OVEN MITTS

FYI
If you don't have buttermilk, you can DIY your own by combining 1 cup milk with 1 tablespoon lemon juice or white vinegar, and letting it sit on the counter for 10 minutes. Use immediately!

DONUT SHAKES

Makes 2 shakes

My family has a donut-shop tradition. We never eat just one donut. Especially the dads in the family. When we roll up to the donut shop, we go big. One donut for now, one donut to take home for later. When I really want to make a dad feel special, I bust out donut #2 and blend it with whatever ice cream I have on hand, for a "breakfast for dessert" treat. Hint: Dads *love* breakfast in bed. So do moms and sisters and brothers and grandmas and best friends.

INGREDIENTS

4 large scoops of ice cream, flavor of choice

½ cup milk

1 regular donut or 4 mini donuts (we like glazed, but any flavor will do)

COMBINE AND BLEND!

Combine the ice cream, milk, and donut in a blender and blend for 45 seconds, or until you reach your preferred thickness.

DRINK UP!

Pour into glasses and have a blast. (Beware of brain freeze if you drink too quickly!)

EQUIPMENT

ICE CREAM/COOKIE
    SCOOP

MEASURING CUP

BLENDER

2 TALL GLASSES

DECORATE YOUR OWN DONUTS: SPRINKLES, GLAZES . . . GET AFTER IT!

SNAP CRACKLE POP SHAKES

Makes 2 shakes

When fireworks come shooting out of the sky July 4, I'm always trying to find a dessert to match the bombastic noise and energy of the holiday. And, when it comes to dessert, I don't like to compromise—when I am faced with the choice between a Rice Krispie treat and a bowl of ice cream, you better believe I am going to find a way to have both. Enter the Snap Crackle Pop Shake! It's a crowd-pleaser for any and every celebration (fireworks not included).

INGREDIENTS

½ cup mini marshmallows

¼ cup chocolate syrup

4 large scoops of chocolate ice cream

½ cup Rice Krispies cereal

MELT!

In a microwave-safe cup, zap the marshmallows and chocolate syrup for 30 seconds. The marshmallows will puff up and melt together with the chocolate syrup.

COMBINE AND BLEND!

In a blender, mix the marshmallow-chocolate mixture, the chocolate ice cream, and Rice Krispies for 30 seconds, leaving the cereal pieces partially intact.

DRINK UP!

Pour into glasses and have a blast. (Beware of brain freeze if you drink too quickly!)

EQUIPMENT

MICROWAVE + MICROWAVE-SAFE
   CUP

MEASURING CUPS

BLENDER

ICE CREAM/COOKIE SCOOP

2 TALL GLASSES

CORNBREAD

Makes one loaf, 12 slices

One of the best things about summer is corn on the cob. Slathered in butter and impossible to eat without making a mess, it is easily my favorite vegetable. After I had my first ear, I knew that I had to find more ways to get this salty-sweet dream veg into my life on a regular basis. Baking corn kernels into a sliceable loaf means I can have corny goodness anytime—for lunch, served with a melty piece of cheese on top, or as a snack with a dollop of grape butter.

INGREDIENTS

2½ cups flour

½ cup yellow cornmeal

1 tablespoon + 1½ teaspoons baking powder

2¼ teaspoons kosher salt

¾ stick (6 tablespoons) unsalted butter, melted

1 cup + 2 tablespoons sugar

3 eggs

1 cup milk

¾ cup vegetable oil

SERVING

Grape butter (recipe follows)

PREP!

Preheat the oven to 350°F and coat the loaf pan with baking spray.

MIX THE DRY!

In a large bowl, combine the flour, cornmeal, baking powder, and salt.

WHISK THE WET AND COMBINE!

In a medium bowl, whisk the butter and sugar together until combined. Whisk in the eggs, then whisk in the milk and oil. Whisk the wet ingredients into the dry ingredients until smooth.

POUR AND BAKE!

Pour the batter into the prepared loaf pan and bake at 350°F for 55 to 60 minutes, until a toothpick comes out clean when poked into the center of the loaf (see page 23). Using oven mitts, remove the loaf pan from the oven and let the cake cool completely in the pan. Slice and serve with a dollop of grape butter. Store on the counter in an airtight container for up to 1 week.

EQUIPMENT

OVEN

9 BY 5-INCH LOAF PAN

BAKING SPRAY

MIXING BOWLS

MEASURING CUPS + SPOONS

WHISK

TOOTHPICK

OVEN MITTS

BUTTER KNIFE

HAND MIXER OR STAND MIXER WITH
  PADDLE ATTACHMENT

GRAPE BUTTER

Makes about ½ cup

INGREDIENTS

1 stick (8 tablespoons) unsalted butter

3 tablespoons grape jelly

WHIP!

In the bowl of a stand mixer (or in a mixing bowl using a hand mixer), combine the butter and grape jelly. Whip on medium speed for 2 minutes, until combined and fluffy. Serve at room temperature or store in the fridge for up to 1 week.

RUFFLES HAVE RRRIDGES!™

peaches
and cream
smoothies

all-the-fruit
smoothies

PEACHES AND CREAM SMOOTHIES

Makes 2 smoothies

My family is always trying to get me to eat fresh fruit in the summer. But sometimes it feels so boring. Plus, I like to wake up and go play with my friends, not sit at the breakfast table. I love this combo *so* much, I find myself eating it year-round. It's especially great on the go.

FYI
If you have other fruit you love to eat and think it will taste great with yogurt, put it in the freezer the night before and go for it!

INGREDIENTS

8 frozen peach slices

¼ cup vanilla yogurt

½ cup orange juice

COMBINE AND BLEND!

Combine the peach slices, yogurt, and orange juice in a blender and blend for 45 seconds, or until you reach your preferred thickness.

DRINK UP!

Pour into glasses and have a blast.

EQUIPMENT

MEASURING CUPS

BLENDER

2 TALL GLASSES

ALL-THE-FRUIT SMOOTHIES

Makes 2 smoothies

This could also be titled the "Christina, You-Want-a-Smoothie-but-You-Don't-Want-to-Think-Too-Much-About-It-So-Just-Open-the-Fridge-and-Blend-Up-Any-Fruit-You-Find-in-It Smoothie," but that's just a little too long. Whether I just got back from berry picking with my family or I picked up some fruit at the grocery, this berry-OJ combo is my fave—but then, I'm *always* in for a smoothie experiment.

FYI
Fresh fruit works great here, but if you're using fresh fruit, add ½ cup ice cubes to keep your smoothie thick and cold.

INGREDIENTS

2 cups frozen or fresh strawberries

¼ cup frozen or fresh raspberries

½ cup frozen or fresh blueberries

¼ cup orange juice

COMBINE AND BLEND!

Combine the berries and juice in a blender and blend for 45 seconds, or until you reach your preferred thickness.

DRINK UP!

Pour into glasses and have a blast.

EQUIPMENT

MEASURING CUPS

BLENDER

2 TALL GLASSES

BERRIES AND CREAM MUFFINS

Makes 12 muffins

Summer is not a time to be spent around the kitchen table, eating a slow breakfast. Summer is time for family vacations, playdates and pal-ing around. School is out, the sun is shining, the birds are chirping, and you need . . . need to get out there and chase life down. Summer is also when berries are at their best! Bake these blueberry and creamy white chocolate chip muffins the night before, and grab one on your way out the door the next morning. A breakfast on the go, the muffin will fuel you as you ride your bike as fast as you can, cannonball off the high dive (give yourself 20 minutes to digest!), or organize an epic hide-and-go-seek tournament. On second thought, maybe grab two muffins.

FYI

If you don't have buttermilk, you can DIY your own by combining ½ cup milk with ½ tablespoon lemon juice or white vinegar, and letting it sit on the counter for 10 minutes. This will give you more than enough for this recipe. Use immediately!

AUGUST

INGREDIENTS

3 cups flour

1 tablespoon baking powder

½ teaspoon baking soda

½ teaspoon kosher salt

2 eggs

1 cup sugar

½ cup buttermilk

1 teaspoon vanilla extract

1 cup vegetable oil

1 cup fresh blueberries

1 cup white chocolate chips

EQUIPMENT

OVEN

12-CUP CUPCAKE/MUFFIN PAN

12 PAPER CUPCAKE LINERS

MIXING BOWLS

MEASURING CUPS + SPOONS

WHISK

RUBBER SPATULA

TOOTHPICK

OVEN MITTS

PREP!

Preheat the oven to 375°F. Line the cups of the muffin pan with the cupcake liners.

MIX THE DRY!

In a large bowl, combine the flour, baking powder, baking soda, and salt.

WHISK THE WET AND COMBINE!

In a medium bowl, whisk together the egg, sugar, buttermilk, and vanilla. Whisk in the oil.

Add the wet ingredients to the dry ingredients and whisk until smooth. Stir in the blueberries and white chocolate chips.

SCOOP AND BAKE!

Using a measuring cup, spoon ⅓ cup of the batter into each muffin cup. The batter will fill to right up under the lip of the liner (but shouldn't go over!). Bake at 375°F for 18 to 20 minutes, until the tops brown slightly and a toothpick comes out clean when poked into the center of a muffin (see page 23). With oven mitts, take the pan out of the oven. Let the muffins cool in the pan. These will last in an airtight container on your counter for 4 or 5 days.

CORN DOG WAFFLES

Makes 4 waffles

The highlight of my summers has always been the county fair. I love the dizzying combination of swirly rides, flashing lights, mega slides, and all the fried foods you can imagine. I would beg my mom to take me as soon as the fair hit town. While I can think of no better meal than a corn dog for dinner and a funnel cake for dessert, the fair comes to town only once a year, so I dreamt up these corn dog waffles as a way to live my fair dreams the other fifty-one weeks of the year.

INGREDIENTS

1 cup yellow cornmeal

1 cup flour

¼ cup sugar

1 tablespoon + 1 teaspoon baking powder

1 teaspoon kosher salt

¾ cup milk

2 eggs

⅓ cup vegetable oil

3 hot dogs, cut in half lengthwise, then into ¼-inch pieces

SERVING

¼ cup yellow mustard

PREP!

Turn on the waffle maker and set it to medium heat.

WHISK THE DRY!

In a medium bowl, whisk together the cornmeal, flour, sugar, baking powder, and salt.

WHISK THE WET AND COMBINE!

In a small bowl, whisk together the milk, egg, and oil. Pour this wet mixture into the flour mixture and whisk until your pancake batter is mostly smooth. Stir in the hot dog pieces.

COOK!

Pour ½ cup of the batter—or the amount your waffle maker suggests—onto the waffle maker, smoothing it slightly. Cover and cook for about 2 minutes, or until cooked through. Remove from the waffle maker using the spatula and keep warm while you make the rest of the waffles.

SERVE!

Serve warm, with mustard for dipping.

EQUIPMENT

WAFFLE MAKER

MIXING BOWLS

MEASURING CUPS + SPOONS

WHISK

PLASTIC SPATULA

PURPLE COW FLOATS

Makes 2 floats

Ever had a root beer float? How about a Coke float? I'll take one of each anytime. But did you know there's a world of floats waiting for you beyond those? Also, did you know it's mandatory to consume twice as much ice cream in summertime as in any other season? In the world of floats—cool, creamy ice cream floating like an island in a soda pop sea—anything goes. You just need to make sure it has a *killer* name. In this case, purple = grape soda, cow = vanilla ice cream, float = the magic that happens when you combine the two!

FYI
If you're not a soda drinker, no worries! Vanilla ice cream in a sea of orange juice, or chocolate ice cream in cherry juice, is every bit as fun and tasty! But I'll leave the naming of those floats up to you.

INGREDIENTS
4 large scoops of vanilla ice cream

1½ cups grape soda

SCOOP AND ADD!
Place 2 scoops of ice cream into each large glass, top with soda, and watch the ice cream float to the top.

DRINK UP!
Serve with a spoon and a straw.

MAKE YOUR OWN KILLER FLOAT, AND GIVE IT A NAME!

| _____ | + | _____ | = | _____ |
| (color) | | (animal) | | (your new creation!) |

| _____ | + | _____ | = | _____ |
| (pattern) | | (flower) | | (your new creation!) |

| _____ | + | _____ | = | _____ |
| (funny word) | | (family member name) | | (your new creation!) |

EQUIPMENT
ICE CREAM/COOKIE SCOOP

MEASURING CUPS

2 TALL GLASSES

SPOONS AND STRAWS

BACON-CHEDDAR CORNBAKE MUFFINS

FYI
Bake and eat these puppies right away; they aren't as special on day 2.

AUGUST

Makes 6 muffins

Cornbake is my family's signature dish. It's like cornbread mixed with corn pudding. We serve it on holidays and any old time really. It is salty and a little sweet and corny, and always disappears quickly. We like to think it's perfect already, but very few things can't be improved upon by wrapping them in bacon and making them even easier to eat. Thus, we have I bacon-cheddar cornbake *muffin*. If you want to make this *your* signature dish, I won't stop you.

INGREDIENTS

9 slices of bacon

¾ cup flour

3 tablespoons yellow cornmeal

1½ teaspoons baking powder

¼ teaspoon kosher salt

1 egg

⅓ cup milk

¼ cup sugar

¼ cup vegetable oil

2 tablespoons unsalted butter, melted

½ (15-ounce) can of corn kernels, drained

¾ cup shredded cheddar cheese

EQUIPMENT

OVEN

12-CUP CUPCAKE/MUFFIN PAN

BAKING SPRAY

MICROWAVE + MICROWAVE-SAFE
  PLATE

MIXING BOWLS

MEASURING CUPS + SPOONS

WHISK

RUBBER SPATULA

TOOTHPICK

OVEN MITTS

PREP!

Preheat the oven to 400°F. Coat 6 cups of a 12-cup muffin pan with baking spray.

ZAP!

Stack 3 pieces of paper toweling on a microwave-safe plate. Place 4 or 5 pieces of bacon on the towels (making sure they don't touch) and then cover with another 2 pieces of paper towels. Microwave for 2 minutes, until the bacon is mostly cooked but not yet crispy. Repeat with the remaining slices.

MIX THE DRY AND COMBINE!

In a large bowl, combine the flour, cornmeal, baking powder, and salt.

WHISK THE WET AND COMBINE!

In a medium bowl, whisk together the egg, milk, and sugar. Whisk in the oil and melted butter.

Add the wet ingredients to the dry ingredients and whisk until smooth. Stir in the corn.

BACON TIME!

Use a full piece of bacon to line the sides of 6 cups of your prepared muffin pan (around the inside rim), then use half a piece of bacon to line the bottoms of each. Make sure the bottom piece of bacon touches the top piece.

SCOOP AND BAKE!

Using a measuring cup, scoop ⅓ cup of the batter into the bacon-lined muffin cups. Top each cup of batter with 2 tablespoons of the shredded cheese. Bake at 400°F for 22 minutes, until the muffin tops brown slightly and a toothpick comes out clean when poked into the center of a muffin (see page 23). With oven mitts, take the pan out of the oven and let the muffins cool slightly in the pan for 3 minutes, then pop out of the pan and serve warm.

STRAWBERRY SHORTCAKES

Makes 9 shortcakes

These all-time faves of mine are a bit like a pig wearing a bow tie: At first glance they seem fancy and maybe even intimidating, but once you get to know them a little, you realize they are just playing dress up! Made with simple ingredients and easy to whip up in a flash, these fluffy cakes, when served with macerated (aka sweet and soupy) strawberries and whipped sour cream, are the perfect last-minute dessert when a barnyard animal in formal wear shows up for dinner—or if you just happen to have some strawberries on hand.

INGREDIENTS

1¾ cups flour

½ cup sugar

⅓ cup packed light brown sugar

2 teaspoons baking powder

2 teaspoons kosher salt

1 egg

¼ cup heavy cream

1½ sticks (12 tablespoons) unsalted butter, cold, cut into ¼-inch cubes

1 cup powdered sugar

SERVING

1 recipe (3 cups) macerated strawberries (recipe follows)

1 recipe (1¾ cups) whipped sour cream (recipe follows)

PREP!

Preheat the oven to 350°F and coat the baking sheet with baking spray.

MIX!

In a large bowl, mix the flour, both sugars, baking powder, and salt. Crack the egg into a small bowl and whisk it thoroughly with the cream.

TOSS AND PINCH!

Add the butter to the dry ingredients and pinch the butter pieces with your fingers, working the dough until you no longer see pieces of butter, about 2 minutes (see page 203, pictures 1 and 2). You will have a shaggy mixture.

STREAM THE CREAM!

Add the cream mixture to the flour-butter mixture. Stir gently with a wooden spoon until the cream is incorporated, about 30 seconds. Let the dough rest for 5 minutes in the bowl.

WAITING FOR THE DOUGH!

While your shortcake dough is resting, skip ahead and make the macerated strawberries and whipped soured cream.

EQUIPMENT

OVEN

BAKING SHEET

BAKING SPRAY

MIXING BOWLS

MEASURING CUPS + SPOONS

WHISK

BUTTER KNIFE

WOODEN SPOON

ICE CREAM/COOKIE SCOOP OR LARGE SPOON

OVEN MITTS

(recipe continues)

SCOOP, ROLL, AND BAKE!

Scoop the dough into 9 balls, using 3 tablespoons of dough to form each ball. Pour the powdered sugar into a bowl and roll each dough ball around in the sugar to coat. Transfer the dough balls to the prepared baking sheet, placing them 2 inches apart. Bake at 350°F for 13 minutes, until golden brown around the edges.

SERVE!

Serve the shortcakes warm or at room temperature with a spoonful of macerated strawberries and a dollop of whipped soured cream. These shorties are best served the day they are made.

WHIPPED SOUR CREAM

Makes 1¾ cups

INGREDIENTS

½ cup heavy cream

½ cup sour cream

3 tablespoons powdered sugar

EQUIPMENT

MIXING BOWL

WHISK

MEASURING CUPS + SPOONS

COMBINE AND WHISK!

In a medium bowl, use a whisk to whip the heavy cream, sour cream, and powdered sugar together, mixing until fluffy. Whisk fast, but not so fast that the cream gets all over the place! If you're used to doing this, it'll take about 2 minutes; if you're still learning, it'll take a little longer, but you can do it!

MACERATED STRAWBERRIES

Makes 3 cups

INGREDIENTS
4 cups fresh strawberries

¼ cup sugar

EQUIPMENT
BUTTER KNIFE

CUTTING BOARD

MIXING BOWL

MEASURING CUPS

SLICE AND COMBINE!

Cut off the leafy tops of the strawberries with a butter knife, then slice the berries on the cutting board. In a large bowl, gently toss the strawberries with the sugar; the sugar will draw out their juices, making for a delicious, liquidy treat. Serve cold or at room temperature, using the liquid as part of the dish by pouring it over the shortcakes and strawberries.

AUGUST

...H

...ack Obama, many

...y ate _____ dog lovers. Here's a

...ECTIVE   TYPE OF FOOD

...Harding once invited neighborhood

...White House for his Airedale terrier's birthday

...d after an Army _____ made of dog biscuits!

... Fala even starred in a/an _____ movie!

...klin Delano Roosevelt's beloved Scottish terrier was

...ee H. W. Bush's springer spaniel published her own

... by the First _____ , which sold more

...Bush's _____ . A few years later, the First Family

...ama received Bo the Portuguese water

... later, the First Family

_____
NOUN

House LLC

BEST CHOCOLATE CHIP COOKIES EVER (TO ME, ANYWAY)

FYI
You want your butter to be soft and melty, not fully liquid and definitely not steaming hot. The best way to do this is in the microwave (in a microwave-safe bowl) on high for 30 seconds. If you need to heat it for longer (some microwaves are stronger than others), do it in 15-second bursts, and take a look at it between zaps.

Makes 18 to 24 cookies

Any day of the week, month, or year is the perfect time for a chocolate chip cookie, but something about its warm, cozy, fresh-from-the-oven goodness makes it perfect for the end of summer. Everyone has his or her own "soul mate" chocolate chip cookie, and this is mine. It is nothing fancy, just crisp on the outside and warm and gooey on the inside—just the way I like my almost fall days.

INGREDIENTS

1¾ cups flour

2 tablespoons nonfat milk powder

1¼ teaspoons kosher salt

½ teaspoon baking powder

¼ teaspoon baking soda

2 sticks (16 tablespoons) unsalted butter, super soft

¾ cup packed light brown sugar

½ cup sugar

1 egg

2 teaspoons vanilla extract

1 (12-ounce) bag chocolate chips

EQUIPMENT

OVEN

2 BAKING SHEETS

BAKING SPRAY

MIXING BOWLS

MEASURING CUPS + SPOONS

WOODEN SPOON OR PLASTIC SPATULA

FRIDGE (OPTIONAL)

ICE CREAM/COOKIE SCOOP

OVEN MITTS

PREP!

Preheat the oven to 350°F. Coat the baking sheets with baking spray.

MIX THE DRY!

In a medium bowl, mix the flour, milk powder, salt, baking powder, and baking soda until well combined.

MIX THE WET AND COMBINE!

In a large bowl, and using a wooden spoon or sturdy spatula, mix the butter and sugars, flexing your muscles for about 2 minutes, until they are fully combined. Add the egg and vanilla and stir until combined and fluffy, about 1 minute. Add the dry mixture to the butter-sugar mixture, mixing until just combined. (If your dough is exceptionally wet—if it looks really shiny or oily—your butter was likely too hot. Throw the dough in the fridge for a few minutes to firm up before continuing on.)

CHOCOLATE TIME!

Stir in the chocolate chips.

SCOOP AND BAKE!

Scoop your dough into balls 2 tablespoons in size and place them 2 to 3 inches apart onto the prepared baking sheets. Bake at 350°F for 10 to 12 minutes, until the edges of the cookies are golden brown. With oven mitts, remove the baking sheets from the oven and cool the cookies completely on the baking sheets. Store in an airtight container for up to 1 week.

FYI
The secret ingredient in these cookies is the milk powder; read up on it on page 19.

CINNAMON SUGAR AND PEACH SHORTCAKES

Makes 9 shortcakes

End-of-summer checklist:

- ❏ Make an epic, block-long hopscotch court
- ❏ Cannonball off the high dive
- ❏ Turn the backyard into a national park and camp for a night
- ❏ Hit a home run—or at least steal a base or two
- ❏ Have one last Slip 'N Slide session
- ☑ Bake a batch of the fluffiest shortcakes, with gooey cinnamon peaches on the side

INGREDIENTS

1¾ cups flour

½ cup sugar

⅓ cup packed light brown sugar

2 teaspoons baking powder

2 teaspoons kosher salt

1 teaspoon ground cinnamon, plus ½ teaspoon for rolling

1 egg

¼ cup heavy cream

1½ sticks (12 tablespoons) unsalted butter, cold, cut into ¼-inch cubes (yes, that's tiny, but you can do it!)

1 cup powdered sugar

SERVING

Gooey peaches (recipe follows)

Vanilla whipped cream (recipe follows)

PREP!
Preheat the oven to 350°F and coat the baking sheet with baking spray.

MIX THE DRY!
In a large bowl, mix the flour, sugars, baking powder, salt, and 1 teaspoon cinnamon.

CRACK AND WHISK!
Crack the egg into a small bowl and whisk it thoroughly with the cream.

TOSS AND PINCH!
Add the butter to the dry ingredients and pinch with your fingers, working until you no longer see pieces of butter, about 2 minutes. You will have a shaggy mixture.

STREAM THE CREAM!
Add the cream mixture. Stir gently with a wooden spoon until all is mixed well, about 30 seconds. Let the dough rest for 5 minutes in the bowl.

WAITING FOR THE DOUGH!
While your shortcake dough is resting, skip ahead and make the gooey peaches and vanilla whipped cream.

EQUIPMENT

OVEN

BAKING SHEET

BAKING SPRAY

MIXING BOWLS

MEASURING CUPS + SPOONS

WHISK

BUTTER KNIFE

WOODEN SPOON

ICE CREAM/COOKIE SCOOP
   OR LARGE SPOON

OVEN MITTS

(recipe continues)

SCOOP AND ROLL!

Scoop out 3 tablespoons of dough and shape into a ball. Continue to make balls of dough. Pour the powdered sugar and remaining ½ teaspoon cinnamon in a bowl, and roll each dough ball around in the cinnamon sugar to coat well. Transfer the dough balls to the prepared baking sheet, placing them about 2 inches apart.

BAKE!

Bake at 350°F for 13 minutes, until golden brown at the edges. With oven mitts, remove the baking sheet from the oven and let the shortcakes cool briefly on the baking sheet, then transfer to plates.

SERVE!

Serve the shortcakes still warm or at room temperature, along with a spoonful of gooey peaches and a dollop of whipped cream. These are best served right away, but you can also stash them in an airtight container for up to 3 days.

SEPTEMBER

GOOEY PEACHES

Makes 1 cup

INGREDIENTS

3 fresh peaches, peeled, pitted, and sliced into ½-inch pieces

¼ cup light brown sugar

1 tablespoon unsalted butter, melted

Pinch of kosher salt

EQUIPMENT

OVEN

CUTTING BOARD

BUTTER KNIFE

BAKING SHEET

MIXING BOWL

MEASURING CUPS + SPOONS

OVEN MITTS

PREP!

Preheat the oven to 350°F.

MIX AND BAKE!

In a medium bowl, mix your peaches, brown sugar, butter, and salt.

Pour the peach mixture onto the baking sheet and bake at 350°F for 5 to 10 minutes (depending on the ripeness of your peaches) until tender. Remove from the oven using oven mitts.

VANILLA WHIPPED CREAM

Makes 1¾ cups

INGREDIENTS

1 cup heavy cream

2 tablespoons powdered sugar

½ teaspoon vanilla extract

EQUIPMENT

MEDIUM MIXING BOWL

MEASURING CUPS + SPOONS

WHISK

WHIP!

In a medium bowl, use a whisk to whip the heavy cream, powdered sugar, and vanilla together, mixing until fluffy. Whisk fast, but not so fast that the cream gets all over the place! If you're used to doing this, it'll take about 2 minutes. If you're still learning, it'll take a little longer, but you can do it!

FYI
If you have leftover scraps of dough after you cut out your cookies, combine them into a ball and roll it o again for more cookies. I the dough gets too sticky chill it in the fridge for 15 minutes.

CUT-OUT COOKIES

Makes 24 cookies, depending on size

Everyone loves an art project. I mean, when else do you get to splatter paint like a maniac and call it a masterpiece? A chunk of clay that you smooshed with your hands? Put it in a museum! These cookies are every bit an excuse to channel your inner artist. They also happen to be a delicious treat. Also, they are very giftable—some may say these are best made for Christmas, but in my book it doesn't need to be a holiday for you to get busy!

FYI
Chilling the dough makes it easier to roll out, *plus* you can easily stash a bag of dough for later.

INGREDIENTS

2 sticks (16 tablespoons) unsalted butter, softened

½ cup packed light brown sugar

2 cups flour, plus more for dusting

½ teaspoon kosher salt

EQUIPMENT

2 BAKING SHEETS

BAKING SPRAY

MIXING BOWL

MEASURING CUPS + SPOONS

WOODEN SPOON OR STAND MIXER WITH PADDLE ATTACHMENT

3 ZIP-TOP PLASTIC BAGS (OR PLASTIC WRAP)

FRIDGE

OVEN

ROLLING PIN

RULER

COOKIE CUTTERS

METAL SPATULA

OVEN MITTS

PREP!
Coat the baking sheets with baking spray.

WHISK AND COMBINE!
In a large bowl, combine the softened butter and brown sugar using a wooden spoon (or in a stand mixer). Mix until the butter and sugar are smooth, about 2 minutes by hand (or 45 seconds in a mixer). Add the flour and salt and stir or mix until smooth (if you're not using a mixer, it may be easiest to ditch the spoon and use your hands to form the dough.)

SHAPE AND CHILL!
Form the dough into a ball, and divide the ball into 3 pieces. Place each piece in a plastic bag and pat the dough smooth and flat with your hands. Refrigerate for 15 minutes. Meanwhile, preheat the oven to 350°F.

ROLL AND CUT!
Dust a clean, dry section of your countertop with flour. Place one batch of the dough down on it and use a flour-dusted rolling pin to roll it out until it is ¼ inch thick (use a ruler!). Use your favorite cookie cutters to cut the dough into shapes. Using a metal spatula, lift the shapes and transfer them to the prepared baking sheets. Repeat with the remaining 2 packages of dough. If you use a range of cookie sizes and shapes, keep the bigger cut-outs on one baking sheet and the smaller cut-outs on the other baking sheet.

BAKE!
Bake the cookies at 350°F for 5 to 10 minutes (depending on the size of your cut-outs), until the edges of the cookies are golden brown. With oven mitts, remove the baking sheets from the oven and cool the cookies completely on the baking sheets.

MAKE THEM YOUR OWN!
Ready to turn your inner Picasso on? Turn to page 144 to see our fave way to decorate!

(recipe continues)

COOKIE GLAZES

A cut-out cookie without a glaze is like a burger without cheese or like popcorn without butter: Fine, but it could really use a little something to take it to the next level. Glazes are my favorite way to bring color and flavor to the canvas that is a cut-out cookie. Once you glaze, you will never go back, trust me.

I'm so mad for glazes that I glaze cakes, cupcakes, muffins, pancakes, and fruit slices. Heck, I'll even glaze a piece of toast. With just two ingredients, glazes could not be simpler to make and are begging to be experimented with. Want to try out a raspberry glaze for your next sandie? Grab some jam! Think your gingerbread cut-out needs a fruity BFF? Splash on some apple juice! Want a mustard glaze to top your chocolate cookie? Okay, maybe we've gone too far....

FYI
If your glaze is too loose, add some powdered sugar until you reach the desired thickness. If your glaze is too dry, add the teeniest, tiniest splash of additional liquid.

OUR FAVORITE FLAVORS

Apple juice

Orange juice

Lemon juice

Root beer

Peanut butter + a splash of milk

Chocolate syrup + a splash of milk

Milk + a splash of vanilla extract

Milk + a splash of mint extract

Strawberry milk

INGREDIENTS

1 tablespoon of liquid (see flavor suggestions at left)

½ cup powdered sugar

Food coloring (optional)

WHISK!

In a small bowl, combine your chosen liquid with the powdered sugar, and whisk until smooth.

GLAZE COOKIES!

See page 144 for our favorite way to glaze and decorate cookies.

P.S.
As is, the glazes have some color, but if you want to turn it up a notch, add a drop or two of food coloring using your desired hue. Just start with one drop and see if you want more—a little goes a long way!

EQUIPMENT

MIXING BOWL

MEASURING CUPS + SPOONS

WHISK

(recipe continues)

GRAB YOUR SMOCKS AND BERETS—ART CLASS IS IN SESSION!

Half the joy of cut-out cookies is eating them, and the other half is decorating them. It's not my style to spend *too* much time on each cookie. Someone will inevitably be devouring your masterpiece, after all! But I like to start with a few small bowls of glazes in different colors and flavors (see page 143), and a few bowls of toppings— sprinkles, chocolate chips, white chocolate chips, and gummy candies work great. From here on, the choice is yours! Dip your cookie straight into the glaze for a smooth layer, or use a spoon to drizzle and spread frosting in your favorite designs and sprinkle on the toppings: The cookie is your canvas! Lay your finished cookies on a parchment paper–lined cookie sheet for a few minutes to dry before sharing.

BONUS: Decorated cut-out cookies make a great gift. Wrap them in a nice tin or fancy up a plain box!

DIY ICE CREAM SANDWICHES

FYI
These sandwiches can be made with your choice of cake and ice cream flavors. We like this combo for OG ice cream sandwich vibes.

Makes 16 sandwiches

Snow cone. Push-up pop. Chocotaco. Fudge bar. Sure, sure, these are all great. But when I hear the jingle-jangle of the ice cream truck and run to grab whatever change I can scrape together from the sofa cushions, there is only one treat I have my eyes on: the classic ice cream sandwich. Haters will say that this timeless treat isn't *that* special, but I know the truth: This vanilla-chocolate combo never disappoints. Now you can whip it up in your own kitchen when the ice cream man is nowhere to be found, or your piggy bank is empty.

SEPTEMBER

2 (9 by 13-inch) thin chocolate cakes, still in baking pans
(recipe follows)

3 cups vanilla ice cream, softened slightly in the microwave

LAYER UP AND CHILL!

Grab one chocolate cake layer, leaving it in its pan. Use your spatula to spread the softened ice cream evenly across the cake layer, getting it into the corners. Remove the second cake from its pan, and place it, top side up, on top of your ice cream layer. Using some force, press the layers together—you want the cake and ice cream sticking together. Place the pan with the layered cake and ice cream in the freezer to set firm, at least 2 hours.

SLICE!

Run a butter knife around the perimeter of the pan to help release the frozen ice cream sandwich from the pan. On a large cutting board, flip the pan upside down and smack the bottom to release the sandwich onto the cutting board. With an adult's help, use a sharp chef's knife to trim and square the edges. Then slice the cake lengthwise in half, cut the cake into 2 rows of 8 rectangles each, for 16 sandwiches—like the classic ice cream sandwich. Serve immediately. These can also be wrapped well in plastic and stored in an airtight container in the freezer for up to 2 weeks. Serve them straight out of the freezer.

EQUIPMENT

MICROWAVE

RUBBER SPATULA

FREEZER

BUTTER KNIFE

CUTTING BOARD

CHEF'S KNIFE

(recipe continues)

THIN CHOCOLATE CAKE

Makes 2 thin cake layers

INGREDIENTS

1¼ cups flour

½ cup cocoa powder

1 tablespoon baking powder

½ teaspoon kosher salt

½ stick (4 tablespoons) unsalted butter, melted

¾ cup sugar

3 tablespoons light brown sugar

2 eggs

½ cup vegetable oil

1½ teaspoons vanilla extract

½ cup buttermilk

PREP!

Preheat the oven to 350°F and coat the baking pans with baking spray.

MIX THE DRY!

In a medium bowl, combine the flour, cocoa powder, baking powder, and salt.

WHISK THE WET AND COMBINE!

In a large bowl, whisk together the butter, both sugars, and the eggs until well combined. Whisk in the oil and vanilla. Whisk in the buttermilk.

Whisk the dry ingredients into the wet ingredients until smooth.

POUR AND BAKE!

Pour half your batter into each of the prepared baking pans and spread evenly with a spatula into all the corners. (If you have only one baking pan, you can bake the cake in two steps; respray and refill the baking pan with cake batter after the first one has cooled.) Bake at 350°F for 5 to 7 minutes, until set and bouncy to the touch. Using oven mitts, remove both pans from the oven, and let the cake layers cool completely in the pan.

SEPTEMBER

FYI
If you don't have buttermilk, you can DIY your own by combining ½ cup milk with ½ tablespoon lemon juice or white vinegar, and letting it sit on the counter for 10 minutes. Use immediately!

EQUIPMENT

OVEN

TWO 9 BY 13-INCH BAKING PANS

BAKING SPRAY

MIXING BOWLS

MEASURING CUPS + SPOONS

WHISK

RUBBER SPATULA

OVEN MITTS

cherry pie cereal squares, opposite

compost cereal squares, page 152

CHERRY PIE CEREAL SQUARES

FYI
Swap the dried cherries or cereal for whatever you love most (or whatever you've got in the cupboard)!

Makes 15 squares

A staple on diner menus across the country, cherry pie is often overlooked for its blueberry and apple brothers and sisters, which is just *bananas* in my book. All fruit puns aside, this cherry-studded treat plays second fiddle to no one.

INGREDIENTS

5 tablespoons unsalted butter (save the paper it's wrapped in!)

1 (10.5-ounce) bag marshmallows

1 cup dried cherries

6 cups Cheerios cereal

PREP!
Coat the baking pan with baking spray.

MELT!
In a very large, microwave-safe bowl, melt the butter and marshmallows together for 2 minutes. Remove from the microwave and stir, then microwave for 1 more minute. Stir until smooth.

ADD MIX-INS!
Stir the dried cherries into the melted marshmallows until well combined.

CEREAL TIME!
Add the Cheerios to the marshmallow mixture and stir with a spatula until every bit is coated.

COOL AND CUT!
Scrape the mixture into the prepared pan and spread evenly with a greased spatula or with the butter paper (my grandma taught me this!). Let cool until firm, 15 to 20 minutes. Then cut to make 3 lengthwise rows and 5 crosswise rows, for a total of 15 treats. Store in an airtight container on your counter for up to 5 days.

FYI
The marshmallows will balloon up in a hilarious way when you microwave them, so make sure you use an oversize bowl.

EQUIPMENT
9 BY 13-INCH BAKING PAN
BAKING SPRAY
MICROWAVE + LARGE MICROWAVE-SAFE BOWL
MEASURING CUPS + SPOONS
RUBBER SPATULA
BUTTER KNIFE

SEPTEMBER

COMPOST CEREAL SQUARES

Makes 9 squares

In the Milk Bar kitchens, Compost has always been a favorite flavor combo. No one is *ever* mad when you combine pretzels, potato chips, butterscotch chips, chocolate chips, and graham crackers together in one bite. It is salty and sweet and unexpected and delicious. One way to make that party even better is to add some cereal and marshmallows. These are enjoyable twelve months of the year, but I find they reach the peak of delicious when eaten outdoors, as the dessert in your picnic basket or in a tent under the stars.

FYI
Due to to certain delicious ingredients, these cereal treats are weighted down more than most, which is why for this recipe I recommend using an 8-inch square pan. A 9 by 13-inch pan will work, but your treats will be much shorter than what I consider optimal cereal square height.

INGREDIENTS

5 tablespoons unsalted butter (save the paper it's wrapped in!)

1 (10.5-ounce) bag marshmallows

1 cup lightly broken up potato chips

1 cup lightly broken-up pretzels

½ cup old-fashioned rolled oats

½ cup chocolate chips

¼ cup butterscotch chips

5 cups Rice Krispies cereal

EQUIPMENT

8-INCH BAKING PAN

BAKING SPRAY

MICROWAVE + LARGE MICROWAVE-
   SAFE BOWL

MEASURING CUPS + SPOONS

RUBBER SPATULA

BUTTER KNIFE

PREP!

Coat the baking pan with baking spray.

MELT!

In a very large microwave-safe bowl, melt the butter and marshmallows together for 2 minutes. Remove from the microwave and stir, then microwave for 1 more minute. Stir until smooth.

ADD MIX-INS!

Stir the potato chips, pretzels, oats, chocolate chips, and butterscotch chips into the melted marshmallows. The chocolate and butterscotch chips will melt and coat everything. This is the best part!

CEREAL TIME!

Add the Rice Krispies to the marshmallow mixture and stir with a spatula until every bit is coated.

SPREAD AND COOL!

Scrape the mixture into the prepared pan and spread evenly with a greased spatula or with the butter paper (my grandma taught me this!). Let cool until firm, 15 to 20 minutes. Then cut into 3 rows one way, then turn the pan and cut 3 rows in the other direction, to make a total of 9 squares. Store in an airtight container on your counter for up to 5 days.

FYI
Swap the cereal and any of the other salty-sweet mix-ins for whatever you love most (or whatever you've got in the cupboard)!

FLUFFERNUTTER COOKIE SANDWICHES

Makes 12 cookie sandwiches

I don't know what crazy sandwich genius first thought of combining Marshmallow Fluff—a tub of gooey, spreadable marshmallows—with glorious peanut butter, making the world-famous Fluffernutter Sandwich, but I'd like to give that person one million high-fives. Because I love it so, I decided to raise the stakes. I swapped out the sandwich bread for my favorite cut-out cookies because I believe everything is better with cookies involved. The fluff guarantees that this treat will stick to the roof of your mouth, but I promise you that is a good thing!

1½ cups Marshmallow Fluff

1 batch (24) cut-out cookies (recipe follows)**, made with 2-inch round cutter**

1½ cups peanut butter

STACK!

Spread a 2-tablespoon dollop of marshmallow on the bottom of one of your cookies. Smooth it with the back of a dinner spoon to make an even layer. Spread a 2-tablespoon dollop of peanut butter on the bottom of one of your other cookies. Smooth it with the back of a dinner spoon to make an even layer. Press together your peanut butter and marshmallow layers, squeezing just until both fillings start to ooze to the edge of the cookie. Repeat with the remaining cookies. Store in an airtight container on the counter for up to 1 week, or in the freezer for up to a month; they're pretty awesome frozen!

(recipe continues)

CUT-OUT COOKIES

Makes 24 cookies

SEPTEMBER

INGREDIENTS

2 sticks (16 tablespoons) unsalted butter, softened

½ cup packed light brown sugar

2 cups flour, plus more for dusting

½ teaspoon kosher salt

> **FYI**
> Chilling the dough makes it easier to roll out, *plus* you can easily stash a bag of dough for later.

EQUIPMENT

2 BAKING SHEETS

BAKING SPRAY

MIXING BOWL

MEASURING CUPS + SPOONS

WOODEN SPOON OR STAND MIXER WITH PADDLE ATTACHMENT

3 ZIP-TOP BAGS (OR PLASTIC WRAP)

FRIDGE

OVEN

ROLLING PIN

RULER

2-INCH ROUND COOKIE CUTTER

METAL SPATULA

OVEN MITTS

PREP!

Coat the baking sheets with baking spray.

COMBINE!

In a large bowl, combine the butter and sugar using a wooden spoon (or in a stand mixer). Mix until the butter and sugar are smooth, about 2 minutes by hand (or 45 seconds in a mixer). Add the flour and salt and stir or mix until smooth (if you're not using a mixer, it may be easiest to ditch the spoon and use your hands to form the dough).

SHAPE AND CHILL!

Form the dough into a ball, and divide the ball into 3 pieces. Place each piece in a plastic bag and pat the dough smooth and flat with your hands. Refrigerate for 15 minutes. Meanwhile, preheat the oven to 350°F.

> **FYI**
> This dough will come out slightly drier than the other cut-out cookies; no worries, as it was made to be this way!

> **FYI**
> If you have leftover scraps of dough after you cut out your cookies, combine them into a ball and roll it out again for more cookies. If the dough gets too sticky, chill it in the fridge for 15 minutes.

ROLL AND CUT!

Dust a clean, dry section of your countertop with a little flour. Take a piece of dough out of the plastic bag and place on the counter. Dust the rolling pin with a little flour and roll out the dough until it is ¼ inch thick (use a ruler!). Use the 2-inch round cutter to cut the dough into 8 cookies. Using a metal spatula, lift the shapes and transfer them to the prepared baking sheets. Repeat with the remaining 2 packages of dough, for a total of 24 cookies.

BAKE!

Bake the cookies at 350°F for 7 to 9 minutes, until the edges of the cookies are golden brown. With oven mitts, remove the baking sheets from the oven and cool the cookies completely on the baking sheets.

ANYTHING GOES SHAKES

Makes 2 shakes

The thing about shakes is that if you mix pretty much anything with ice cream and milk, it is sure to be a hit. May Day! May Day! If you are experiencing a milkshake craving, but don't have whatever you happen to need for a particular recipe, you can still roll up your sleeves and get creative. My basic math is is: ice cream + a little milk + a little something with flavor + something with some crunch = a great shake. The only limit to your shake-ability is your imagination, so get after it! Here are some of my favorites:

- **Mint gelato + almond milk + chocolate fudge + cookie crumbs**

- **Strawberry ice cream + whole milk + caramel sauce + pretzels**

- **Chocolate sorbet + macadamia milk + raspberry jam + almonds**

INGREDIENTS

4 large scoops of ice cream, sorbet, or gelato

¼ cup milk of choice (dairy, almond, soy, macadamia nut, or whatever you've got)

2 tablespoons flavor of choice (peanut butter, almond butter, hazelnut spread, jam, maple syrup, chocolate fudge, caramel sauce, or anything you love)

½ cup texture (nuts, cereal, pretzels, chips, or cookies)

COMBINE AND BLEND!

Combine the ice cream, milk, flavor, and texture elements in a blender and blend for 45 seconds, or until you reach your preferred thickness.

DRINK UP!

Pour into glasses and have a blast.

EQUIPMENT

ICE CREAM/COOKIE SCOOP

MEASURING CUPS + SPOONS

BLENDER

2 TALL GLASSES

FLOWER POWER SMOOTHIES

Makes 2 smoothies

Imagine this: It's back-to-school time, you're faced with a big bowl of fruit, and the thought of eating it all is bananas (even though you do want to make Mom, Dad, or your dog, Oscar, proud). But eating fruit can make you feel bright and powerful. And you can try throwing it all in a blender, splash in some OJ, and 45 seconds later guarantee you will high-fiving Oscar as you slurp up those grapes! Drinking one of these makes me feel like I'm in a video game and I picked up the Flower Power—invincible!

INGREDIENTS

1 cup red grapes, frozen

1 orange, peeled and separated (no seeds!)

2 tablespoons orange juice

COMBINE AND BLEND!

Combine the frozen grapes, orange sections, and orange juice in a blender and blend for 45 seconds, or until you reach your preferred thickness.

DRINK UP!

Pour into glasses and power up!

SMOOTHIE STORY!

_____ 1 _____ says that breakfast is the

_____ 2 _____ meal of the day—I say _____ 3 _____

I've got to go _____ 4 _____ ! If I have to eat

_____ 5 _____ and _____ 6 _____ at least give me a

_____ 7 _____ straw! _____ 8 _____

1 friend's name

2 word that ends in "-est"

3 exclamation

4 your favorite activity to do outside

5 fruit

6 juice

7 color

8 way to say "goodbye"

EQUIPMENT

MEASURING CUPS + SPOONS

BLENDER

2 TALL GLASSES

APPLE PIE WAFFLES

Makes 3 waffles

As soon as fall hits, I beg my BFFs, family, neighbors, dog, and anyone else who will listen to go apple picking with me. I bribe them with promises of cinnamon sugar–covered donuts, hayrides, and warm cider. Once we roll up to the orchard, it is GAME ON, and I won't stop till my satchel is bursting. Everyone knows, the picker with the most apples wins. But my competitive streak also means that I need to get creative with ways to use my abundance of apples. Turns out, that's the only excuse I need to make apple pie for breakfast. Victory never tasted so sweet.

INGREDIENTS

¾ cup flour

¼ cup light brown sugar

1 tablespoon + 1 teaspoon baking powder

1 teaspoon kosher salt

¾ cup milk

1 egg

3 tablespoons vegetable oil

1 cup broken-up graham crackers, vanilla wafers, or shortbread (in penny-size chunks)

SERVING

1 batch gooey cinnamon apples (recipe follows)

1 batch whipped sour cream (recipe follows)

PREP!

Turn on the waffle maker and set it to medium heat.

WHISK THE DRY!

In a medium bowl, whisk together the flour, brown sugar, baking powder, and salt.

WHISK THE WET AND COMBINE!

In a small bowl, whisk together the milk, egg, and oil. Pour this into the dry mixture and whisk until your pancake batter is mostly smooth. Stir in the crackers or cookies.

COOK!

Pour ½ cup of the batter—or the amount your waffle maker suggests—into the middle of the waffle maker, smoothing it slightly. Cook for about 2 minutes, or until cooked through. Remove with the spatula and keep warm while you make the remaining waffles.

SERVE!

Top the waffles with a scoop of gooey cinnamon apples and a dollop of whipped sour cream. Serve immediately.

EQUIPMENT

WAFFLE MAKER

MIXING BOWLS

MEASURING CUPS + SPOONS

WHISK

PLASTIC SPATULA

(recipe continues)

GOOEY CINNAMON APPLES

Makes about 1 cup

SEPTEMBER

INGREDIENTS

2 medium apples, peeled, cored, and cut into small cubes

⅔ cup light brown sugar

½ teaspoon ground cinnamon

Pinch of kosher salt

2 tablespoons unsalted butter, cut into small cubes

EQUIPMENT

OVEN

MEDIUM MIXING BOWL

MEASURING CUPS + SPOONS

CUTTING BOARD

VEGETABLE PEELER

BUTTER KNIFE

RUBBER SPATULA

BAKING SHEET

OVEN MITTS

PREP AND MIX!

Preheat the oven to 350°F. In a medium bowl, mix the apples, brown sugar, cinnamon, and salt.

BAKE!

Pour the apple mixture onto one corner of your baking sheet—the apples cook better if they aren't too spread out—and top with the cubes of butter. Bake in the oven at 350°F for 10 minutes, until golden and soft. Using oven mitts, remove from the oven and let cool slightly on the pan.

FYI
These gooey cinnamon apples are great with loads of stuff. Throw some on top of your fave vanilla ice cream or fancy up your morning toast!

WHIPPED SOUR CREAM

Makes about 1 cup

INGREDIENTS

¼ cup heavy cream

¼ cup sour cream

2 tablespoons powdered sugar

EQUIPMENT

WHISK

SMALL MIXING BOWL

MEASURING CUPS + SPOONS

COMBINE AND WHISK!

Use a whisk to whip your heavy cream, sour cream, and powdered sugar together, mixing until fluffy. Whisk fast, but not so fast that the cream gets all over the place! If you're used to doing this, it'll take about 2 minutes. If you're still learning, it'll take a little longer, but you can do it!

IT'S TIME FOR A TREASURE HUNT!

Get out your magnifying glasses and find these images throughout this book! Write their page numbers here:

Shooting star: _____

Bubbles: _____

A hungry giraffe: _____

An upside-down smiley: _____

CT (my initials): _____

An orange rabbit: _____

JD's notebook: _____

A blue-haired friend: _____

FYI
Swap out the cereal for whatever you love most (or whatever you've got in the cupboard)!

PB&J CEREAL SQUARES

Makes 9 squares

Pro move: If the boss—aka Mom or Dad—asks you to pack your lunch, reassure them you've got your PB&J locked and loaded, then toss this sticky, salty, sweet creation into your Ninja Turtle lunch box for a midday meal that will leave your tablemates begging to trade. If you are really trying to flex, chocolate milk goes great on the side.

FYI
Due to certain delicious ingredients, these cereal treats are weighted down more than most, which is why I recommend using an 8-inch square pan here. A 9 by 13-inch baking pan will work, but your treats will be much shorter than what I consider optimal height.

INGREDIENTS

5 tablespoons unsalted butter (save the paper it's wrapped in!)

1 (10.5-ounce) bag marshmallows

½ cup peanut butter, or any nut butter

½ cup grape jelly, or any fruit preserve

10 cups Corn Flakes cereal

PREP!
Coat the baking pan with baking spray.

MELT!
In a very large, microwave-safe bowl, melt the butter and marshmallows together for 2 minutes. Remove from the microwave and stir, then microwave for 1 more minute. Stir until smooth.

ADD MIX-INS!
Stir the peanut butter and jelly into the melted marshmallows.

CEREAL TIME!
Add the Corn Flakes to the marshmallow mixture and stir with a spatula until every bit is coated.

SPREAD AND COOL!
Scrape the mixture into the prepared baking pan and spread evenly with a greased spatula or with the butter paper (my grandma taught me this!). Let cool until firm, 15 to 20 minutes, then cut into 3 rows in one direction, then turn the pan and cut 3 rows in the other direction, for a total of 9 squares. Store in an airtight container on your counter for up to 5 days.

FYI
The marshmallows will balloon up in a hilarious way when you microwave them, so make sure you use an oversize bowl.

EQUIPMENT

8-INCH SQUARE BAKING PAN

BAKING SPRAY

MICROWAVE + LARGE MICROWAVE-SAFE BOWL

MEASURING CUPS + SPOONS

RUBBER SPATULA

BUTTER KNIFE

BLACK AND WHITE CUPCAKES

Makes 12 frosted cupcakes

From my favorite red Converse high-tops to my crazy headscarf collection, I like to squeeze as much color into my life as possible. I firmly believe that pops of blue and purple and yellow and green just make the days more fun. But that's not to say that non-colorful things don't deserve some love. Three cheers for zebras, newspapers, black and white cookies, classic movies, and these tasty, colorless cupcakes! But just because they're not full of color doesn't mean they're not full of tastiness—this classic chocolate cake topped with dreamy vanilla frosting is like a big ka-POW!

1 batch (12) chocolate cupcakes (recipe follows)

1 batch (2 cups) dreamy vanilla frosting (recipe follows)

ASSEMBLE!

Dollop a large spoonful of vanilla frosting—about 2 tablespoons—on top of each cupcake. Use the back side of your spoon to smooth the frosting into an even and fluffy layer. Store in a large airtight container on the counter for up to 3 days or in the fridge for up to 1 week.

(recipe continues)

OCTOBER

CHOCOLATE CUPCAKES

Makes 12 cupcakes

INGREDIENTS

1¼ cups flour

½ cup cocoa powder

1 tablespoon baking powder

½ teaspoon kosher salt

½ stick (4 tablespoons) unsalted butter, melted

¾ cup sugar

3 tablespoons light brown sugar

2 eggs

½ cup vegetable oil

1½ teaspoons vanilla extract

½ cup buttermilk

OCTOBER

PREP!

Preheat the oven to 350°F. Line the cups of the cupcake pan with the cupcake liners.

MIX THE DRY!

In a large bowl, combine the flour, cocoa powder, baking powder, and salt.

WHISK THE WET AND COMBIE!

In a medium bowl, whisk together the butter, both sugars, and the eggs until well combined. Whisk in the oil and vanilla. Whisk in the buttermilk.

Whisk your wet ingredients into the dry ingredients until smooth.

SCOOP AND BAKE!

Use a ¼-cup measure to scoop portions of the batter into the cups of the cupcake pan. The batter will be almost level with the top edge of the cup (but it shouldn't go over!). Bake at 350°F for 15 to 20 minutes, until a toothpick comes out clean when poked into the center of a cupcake (see page 23). Using oven mitts, remove the cupcake pan from the oven and let the cupcakes cool completely in the pan.

FYI
If you don't have buttermilk, you can DIY your own by combining ½ cup milk with ½ tablespoon lemon juice or white vinegar, and letting it sit on the counter for 10 minutes. Use immediately!

EQUIPMENT

OVEN

12-CUP CUPCAKE/MUFFIN PAN

12 PAPER CUPCAKE LINERS

MIXING BOWLS

MEASURING CUPS + SPOONS

WHISK

RUBBER SPATULA

TOOTHPICK

OVEN MITTS

DREAMY VANILLA FROSTING

Makes 2 cups

INGREDIENTS

1½ sticks (12 tablespoons) unsalted butter, softened

2¼ cups powdered sugar

2 tablespoons milk

1½ teaspoons vanilla extract

¼ teaspoon kosher salt

MIX!

Starting on low speed, use the mixer to combine the butter and powdered sugar, 1 minute. Increase the mixer speed to medium and whip until super smooth, about 3 minutes. Turn off the mixer. Use your spatula to scrape down the sides of your bowl well.

ADD AND FLUFF!

Add the milk, vanilla, and salt. Continue mixing until combined and fluffy, about 1 minute.

EQUIPMENT

HAND MIXER OR STAND MIXER WITH
  PADDLE ATTACHMENT

MIXING BOWL

MEASURING CUPS + SPOONS

RUBBER SPATULA

DINNER SPOON

OCTOBER

NUTTY SANDIES

Makes 24 cookies, depending on size

Have you ever seen a squirrel running around the yard, ferociously gathering nuts to save up for the winter? That's basically me anytime these cookies are around. I throw one of these buttery, nutty cookies in my purse, one in my pocket, one in my lunch box, and, okay, a couple in my mouth. I think those squirrels are onto something.

FYI
If you have leftover scraps of dough after you cut out your cookies, combine them into a ball and roll it out anew for more cookies. If the dough gets too sticky, chill it in the fridge for 15 minutes.

OCTOBER

INGREDIENTS

2 sticks (16 tablespoons) unsalted butter, softened

½ cup packed light brown sugar

1 teaspoon vanilla extract

2 cups flour, plus more for dusting

½ teaspoon kosher salt

½ cup finely crushed nuts (we like pistachios!)

EQUIPMENT

2 BAKING SHEETS

BAKING SPRAY

MIXING BOWL

MEASURING CUPS + SPOONS

WOODEN SPOON OR STAND MIXER
   WITH PADDLE ATTACHMENT

3 ZIP-TOP PLASTIC BAGS
   (OR PLASTIC WRAP)

FRIDGE

OVEN

ROLLING PIN

RULER

COOKIE CUTTERS

PLASTIC SPATULA

OVEN MITTS

PREP!
Coat the baking sheets with baking spray.

WHISK AND COMBINE!
In a large bowl, combine the softened butter, brown sugar, and vanilla using a wooden spoon (or in a stand mixer). Mix until the butter and sugar are smooth, about 2 minutes by hand (or 45 seconds in a mixer). Add the flour, salt, and nuts and stir or mix until well combined (if you're not using a mixer, it may be easiest to ditch the spoon and use your hands to form the dough).

SHAPE AND CHILL!
Form the dough into a ball, and divide the ball into 3 pieces. Place each piece in a plastic bag and pat the dough smooth and flat with your hands. Refrigerate the bags for 15 minutes. Meanwhile, preheat the oven to 350°F.

ROLL AND CUT!
Dust a clean, dry section of your countertop with a little flour. Take a piece of dough out of the plastic bag and place on the counter. Dust the rolling pin with a little flour and roll out the dough until it is ¼ inch thick (use a ruler!). Use your favorite cookie cutters to cut the dough into shapes. Using a spatula, lift the shapes and transfer them to the prepared baking sheet. Repeat with the remaining 2 packages of dough. If you use a range of cookie cutter sizes and shapes, keep the bigger cut-outs on one baking sheet and the smaller cut-outs on the other baking sheet.

BAKE!
Bake the cookies at 350°F for 12 to 17 minutes (depending on the size of your cut-outs), until the edges of the cookies are golden brown. With oven mitts, remove the baking sheets from the oven and cool the cookies completely on the baking sheets.

MAKE THEM YOUR OWN!
Ready to get your Picasso on? Turn to page 144 to see our fave way to decorate!

FYI
Chilling the dough makes it easier to roll out, *plus* you can easily stash a bag of dough for later.

GIVE A DOG A BISCUIT

Makes 12 biscuits

Up until this point, this book has been reserved for human recipes, which I do realize is *really* rude to our canine friends. Next time you make a batch of something for your crew, don't forget to make something for your dog pals, too. Pro tip: If you don't have a dog to call your own, throw a few of these in your backpack and you'll have the perfect icebreaker when you come across one.

INGREDIENTS

2 cups flour, plus extra for dusting

½ cup canned pumpkin

¼ cup chicken, beef, or vegetable broth

1 egg

¼ teaspoon ground cinnamon

PREP!
Preheat the oven to 325°F and coat the baking sheet with baking spray.

MIX!
In a large bowl, combine the flour, pumpkin, broth, egg, and cinnamon and mix well, until you're able to knead the dough into a ball.

ROLL AND CUT!
Dust a clean, dry section of your countertop with a little flour. Place the dough on the counter and use a flour-dusted rolling pin to roll it out until it is ½ inch thick (use a ruler!).

Prick the dough all over with a fork. Cut it into bones (or other dog-friendly shapes) with the cookie cutter.

BAKE!
Transfer the biscuits to the prepared baking sheet and bake at 325°F for 25 minutes, or until they are dried out completely. (Larger biscuits may require an additional 5 to 10 minutes of baking.) Remove the biscuits from the oven with oven mitts and let the biscuits completely cool on the baking sheet. The biscuits will last for a month or so if kept in a zip-top bag on the counter.

No dog bone cookie cutter? No prob! Trace this and use it as a guide!

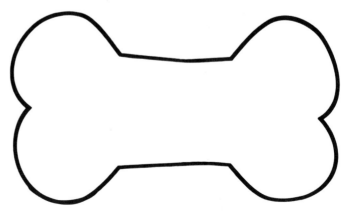

EQUIPMENT
OVEN

BAKING SHEET

BAKING SPRAY

LARGE MIXING BOWL

MEASURING CUPS + SPOONS

WOODEN SPOON

ROLLING PIN

RULER

FORK

BONE-SHAPED COOKIE CUTTER

OVEN MITTS

OCTOBER

PIZZA BREAD

Makes one loaf, 8 or 9 slices

Peanut butter and jelly. Popcorn and butter. Picnics and blankets. Pizza and movie night. Some things just go together, and there is no two ways about it. Every Friday, when I host a movie night—whether it's for just me and my blankets or for a whole crew of folks—I bake this loaf as the main attraction. It's amazing hot out of the oven, and serving it means you don't need to worry about the pizza delivery guy or gal ringing your bell, so you never have to hit pause on the *Back to the Future* marathon to answer the door!

FYI
Every household has their go-to pizza topping, so feel free to use creative liberties for this loaf. No judgments if you are an anchovy-and-olives fan or on the ham-and-pineapple crew.

INGREDIENTS
1 loaf of sandwich bread, 14 slices (we like Italian)

1 (14- or 15-ounce) can pizza sauce or seasoned marinara sauce

2 cups of your favorite toppings (pepperoni, onions, mushrooms, cooked sausage, etc.)

1 (8-ounce) bag shredded pizza Parmesan/mozzarella cheese blend, or more if desired

PREP!
Preheat the oven to 375°F and coat the loaf pan with baking spray.

ROLL AND TOAST!
Roll the bread slices flat and thin with a rolling pin (or flatten them with the palm of your hand). You want the pieces to be wider than what you think will fit into the loaf pan, because they will shrink when toasted. Lay the bread slices on the baking sheets and toast them in the oven for 10 minutes, until dry and slightly golden brown.

BUILD THE STACK!
Line the bottom of the prepared loaf pan with 2 slices of toast so that the entire bottom is covered, then start layering! Build in this order: ¼ cup pizza sauce spread across the top of the bread with a dinner spoon, ¼ cup of your favorite pizza topping, and ¼ cup cheese. Add another layer of toast and repeat. Do this five more times, making your last layer extra cheesy, or throw on some extra topping. Don't be stingy with yourself! Just make sure the last layer is cheese.

BAKE!
Bake your loaf at 375°F for 20 minutes, until the cheese is browning on top and the sauce is bubbling up around it. Using oven mitts, remove the pan from the oven and let the pizza loaf cool slightly in the pan. Remove from the pan, slice into 8 or 9 portions, and serve!

EQUIPMENT
OVEN

9 BY 5-INCH LOAF PAN

BAKING SPRAY

ROLLING PIN (OPTIONAL)

2 BAKING SHEETS

MEASURING CUPS

DINNER SPOON

OVEN MITTS

OCTOBER

POPCORN SHAKES

Makes 2 shakes

I watch the MOST movies in the fall. Probably because it's starting to get cold where I live, and I use it as an excuse to hibernate in front of the TV. The best part of movie night: the snacks. The worst part of movie night: begging mom to hit Pause on *The Fast and the Furious* 'cause you've got buttery popcorn hands. And *then* because you need a bowl of ice cream. And *then* to wash the ice cream dribbles off your pajamas. This shake brings you everything you need for two hours of movie bliss. Just don't forget to make one for Ma!

INGREDIENTS

4 large scoops of vanilla ice cream

½ cup milk

2 cups bagged buttered popcorn

COMBINE AND BLEND!

Combine the ice cream, milk, and popcorn in a blender and blend for 45 seconds, or until you reach your preferred thickness.

DRINK UP!

Pour into glasses and have a blast. (Beware of brain freeze if you drink too quickly!)

OCTOBER

OUR FAVE MOVIE NIGHT PICKS

Singing in the Rain

Rocky (ask your folks first!)

The Karate Kid (1 to 4)

The Sound of Music

Willie Wonka and the Chocolate Factory (the original, please!)

Ghostbusters

Anything from Wes Anderson

Or anything with The Rock!

EQUIPMENT

ICE CREAM/COOKIE SCOOP

MEASURING CUPS

BLENDER

2 TALL GLASSES

popcorn shake,
page 177

pizza bread,
page 176

PUMPKIN PATCH CUPCAKES

Makes 12 frosted cupcakes

Whether you get your pumpkin from the closest grocery store, your local farmers' market, or a full-blown pumpkin patch, everyone acts like carefully selecting the perfect pumpkin is a skill. I take a very non-classic approach to my pumpkin selection: I look for the lopsided, lumpy, barely orange ones. My heart always goes out to the one that I fear no one else will pick up, and the perfect pumpkin is really just a matter of opinion. Beauty is in the eye of the beholder, after all! If you're picking treats, though, these are a no-brainer. Pumpkin frosting on a cinnamon cake, these cupcakes are always the right choice. Stopping at just one, though, is a different trick!

1 batch (12) cinnamon cupcakes (recipe follows)

1 batch (2 cups) pumpkin frosting (recipe follows)

ASSEMBLE!

Dollop about 2 tablespoons of pumpkin frosting on top of each cupcake. Use the back of your spoon to smooth your frosting into an even and fluffy layer. Store in a large airtight container on the counter for up to 3 days or in the fridge for up to 1 week.

(recipe continues)

CINNAMON CUPCAKES

Makes 12 cupcakes

INGREDIENTS

1¾ cups flour

1 tablespoon baking powder

2 teaspoons ground cinnamon

½ teaspoon kosher salt

½ stick (4 tablespoons) unsalted butter, melted

¾ cup sugar

3 tablespoons light brown sugar

2 eggs

½ cup vegetable oil

2 teaspoons vanilla extract

½ cup buttermilk

OCTOBER

PREP!

Preheat the oven to 350°F. Line the cups of the cupcake pan with the cupcake liners.

MIX THE DRY!

In a large bowl, combine the flour, baking powder, cinnamon, and salt.

WHISK THE WET AND COMBINE!

In a medium bowl, whisk together the butter, both sugars, and the eggs until well combined. Whisk in the oil and vanilla. Whisk in the buttermilk.

Whisk your wet ingredients into the dry ingredients until smooth.

SCOOP AND BAKE!

Use a ¼-cup measure to scoop portions of the batter into the cups of the cupcake pan. The batter will be almost level with the top edge of the cup (but it shouldn't go over!). Bake at 350°F for 18 to 20 minutes, until the tops are browned slightly and a toothpick comes out clean when poked into the center of a cupcake (see page 23). Using oven mitts, remove the pan from the oven and cool the cupcakes completely in the pan.

FYI
If you don't have buttermilk, you can DIY your own by combining ½ cup milk with ½ tablespoon lemon juice or white vinegar, and letting it sit on the counter for 10 minutes. Use immediately!

EQUIPMENT

OVEN

12 CUP CUPCAKE/MUFFIN PAN

12 PAPER CUPCAKE LINERS

MIXING BOWLS

MEASURING CUPS + SPOONS

WHISK

RUBBER SPATULA

TOOTHPICK

OVEN MITTS

PUMPKIN FROSTING

Makes 2 cups

INGREDIENTS

2 sticks (16 tablespoons) unsalted butter, softened

2 cups powdered sugar

¼ cup light brown sugar

½ cup canned pumpkin puree

½ teaspoon vanilla extract

½ teaspoon kosher salt

¼ teaspoon ground cinnamon

MIX!

Starting on low speed, use the hand mixer (or a stand mixer) to combine the butter and both sugars, about 1 minute. Increase the mixer speed to medium and whip until super smooth, about 3 minutes. Turn off the mixer. Use your spatula to scrape down the sides of your bowl well.

ADD AND FLUFF!

Add the pumpkin, vanilla, salt, and cinnamon. Continue mixing until combined and fluffy, about 1 minute.

EQUIPMENT

HAND MIXER OR STAND MIXER WITH
  THE PADDLE ATTACHMENT

MIXING BOWL

MEASURING CUPS + SPOONS

RUBBER SPATULA

DINNER SPOON

JACK-O'-LANTERN MUFFINS

Makes 12 muffins

To be honest, during 90 percent of October I am looking forward to crushing fun-size candy bars and inhaling candy corn by the fistful on the 31st. The other 10 percent of the time, I am all about this pumpkin and pumpkin seed–studded muffin. Life is all about balance, right?

INGREDIENTS

2 cups flour

1 tablespoon baking powder

1½ teaspoons cinnamon

¾ teaspoon kosher salt

½ teaspoon baking soda

2 eggs

1½ cups sugar

⅔ cup buttermilk

¼ cup canned pumpkin puree

1 teaspoon vanilla extract

1 cup vegetable oil

1 batch toasted pepitas or pumpkin seeds (recipe follows)

PREP!

Preheat the oven to 375°F. Line the cups of a muffin pan with the cupcake liners.

MIX THE DRY AND COMBINE!

In a large bowl, combine the flour, baking powder, cinnamon, salt, and baking soda.

WHISK THE WET AND COMBINE!

In a medium bowl, whisk together the eggs, sugar, buttermilk, pumpkin puree, and vanilla. Whisk in the oil.

Add the wet ingredients to the dry ingredients and whisk until smooth. Stir in the toasted pepitas.

SCOOP AND BAKE!

Using a measuring cup, spoon ⅓ cup of the batter into each cup in the muffin pan. The batter will come right up under the lip of the liner (but shouldn't go over!). Bake the muffins at 375°F for 18 to 20 minutes, until the muffin tops brown slightly and a toothpick comes out clean when poked into the center of a muffin (see page 23). With oven mitts, take the pan out of the oven and let the muffins cool in the pan. These will last in an airtight container on your counter for 4 or 5 days.

EQUIPMENT

OVEN

BAKING SHEET

12-CUP CUPCAKE/MUFFIN PAN

12 PAPER CUPCAKE LINERS

MIXING BOWLS

MEASURING CUPS + SPOONS

WHISK

RUBBER SPATULA

TOOTHPICK

OVEN MITTS

TOASTED PEPITAS

INGREDIENTS

¼ cup pepitas or pumpkin seeds

PREP!

Preheat the oven to 300°F.

TOAST THE SEEDS!

Spread the pepitas on a dry baking sheet, and toast at 300°F in the oven for 10 minutes, until browned but not burnt. With oven mitts, take them out of the oven and let cool completely.

OCTOBER

TRICK-OR-TREAT QUAKES

Makes 2 quakes

So, you dressed up in a killer costume and hit the streets for an epic trick-or-treat mission—ringing doorbells, stuffing your pillowcases with treats, and earning your sweet reward. Whether you like to ration your candy—having a little of it every day—or crush it all as soon as humanly possible (my move always), this shake helps make your candy stash a fun centerpiece for the season, blended thick and crunchy. In my house, there's candy ready to go into the blender any night of the week.

FYI
At Milk Bar, we love to drink our shakes just fine, but even more so, we love to eat our quakes. The thicker and more luxurious cousin of the shake, the quake requires a spoon—and a hearty appetite.

INGREDIENTS

4 large scoops of ice cream, a little softened (vanilla or chocolate work great)

6 to 8 fun-size chocolate bars or candies of your choosing, plus more for topping

COMBINE AND BLEND!

Combine the ice cream and candies in a blender and blend for 45 seconds, or until you reach your preferred thickness.

DRINK UP!

Pour into glasses and serve with a spoon.

OCTOBER

EQUIPMENT

ICE CREAM/COOKIE SCOOP

BLENDER

2 TALL GLASSES

SPOONS

APPLE-A-DAY CEREAL SQUARES

Makes 9 squares

The saying goes, "An apple a day keeps the doctor away." So by my math, one batch of these apple-studded rectangles will keep you doctor-visit-free for at least twelve years. Sorry, mom, the numbers don't lie.

FYI
Swap the dried fruit if you think a pear or a peach a day will keep the doctor away as well.

INGREDIENTS

5 tablespoons unsalted butter (save the paper it's wrapped in!)

1 (10.5-ounce) bag marshmallows

1 cup freeze-dried apple, broken into small pieces

7 cups Cinnamon Toast Crunch cereal

PREP!
Coat the baking pan with baking spray.

MELT!
In a very large microwave-safe bowl, melt the butter and marshmallows together for 2 minutes. Remove from the microwave and stir, then microwave for 1 more minute. Stir until smooth.

ADD MIX-INS!
Stir the apple bits into the melted marshmallows.

CEREAL TIME!
Add the Cinnamon Toast Crunch to the marshmallow mixture and stir with a spatula until every bit is coated.

SPREAD AND COOL!
Scrape the mixture into the prepared baking pan and spread evenly into the corners with a greased spatula or with the butter paper (my grandma taught me this!). Let cool until firm, 15 to 20 minutes, then cut into 3 rows in one direction, turn the pan, and cut 3 rows in the other direction, to make 9 squares total. Store in an airtight container on your counter for up to 5 days.

FYI
The marshmallows will balloon up in a hilarious way when you microwave them, so make sure you use an oversize bowl.

FYI
Due to certain delicious ingredients, these cereal treats are weighted down more than most, which is why we recommend an 8-inch square pan here. A 9 by 13-inch pan will work, but your treats will be much shorter than what I consider optimal cereal-square height.

EQUIPMENT
MICROWAVE + LARGE MICROWAVE-SAFE BOWL

8-INCH SQUARE BAKING PAN

BAKING SPRAY

RUBBER SPATULA

BUTTER KNIFE

FYI
Swap the cereal for whatever you love most (or whatever you've got in the cupboard)!

FYI
If you like a smaller (or larger) cookie, go for it—you're the boss, after all! Keep in mind that a smaller scoop will bake faster (reduce the bake time by 2 to 4 minutes) and a larger scoop will bake longer (increase the bake time by 2 to 4 minutes).

FYI
You want your butter to be soft and melty, not fully liquid and definitely not steaming hot. The best way to do this is in the microwave (in a microwave-safe bowl) on high for 30 seconds. If you need to heat it for longer (some microwaves are stronger than others), do it in 15-second bursts, and take a look at it between zaps.

LEMONADE ZING COOKIES

Makes 12 to 18 cookies

I have a tip from one businessperson (me) to a potential other one (you): Anyone can run a lemonade stand, but if you are looking to pull in some serious $$$, try a lemon COOKIE stand.

Step 1: Whip up a couple batches of these citrusy crowd-pleasers.

Step 2: Get someone to help you set a table and some chairs in your yard.

Step 3: Advertise. I'm talking flyers taped to telephone poles, a clever jingle you can sing to attract passersby, and maybe get Mom or Dad or Grandma or your older sis to blast it on social media.

Step 4: Start thinking of a way to spend all your profits! My vote: some sick new Rollerblades.

INGREDIENTS

2¼ cups flour

1¼ teaspoons kosher salt

½ teaspoon baking powder

¼ teaspoon baking soda

2 sticks (16 tablespoons) unsalted butter, super soft

1½ cups sugar

1 egg

1 teaspoon lemon extract

1 cup powdered sugar

1 teaspoon powdered lemonade mix

EQUIPMENT

OVEN

2 BAKING SHEETS

BAKING SPRAY

MIXING BOWLS

MEASURING CUPS + SPOONS

WOODEN SPOON OR FIRM RUBBER SPATULA

MICROWAVE + MICROWAVE-SAFE BOWL (OPTIONAL)

FRIDGE (OPTIONAL)

ICE CREAM/COOKIE SCOOP

OVEN MITTS

PREP!

Preheat the oven to 350°F. Coat the baking sheets with baking spray.

MIX THE DRY!

In a medium bowl, mix the flour, salt, baking powder, and baking soda.

MIX THE WET AND COMBINE!

In a large bowl, and using a wooden spoon or sturdy spatula, mix the butter and sugar, flexing your muscles for about 2 minutes, until they are fully combined. Add the egg and lemon extract and stir until combined and fluffy, about 1 minute. Add the dry ingredients to the butter mixture, mixing until just combined. (If your dough is exceptionally wet, your butter was likely too hot. Throw it in the fridge for a few minutes to firm up before continuing on.)

SCOOP AND ROLL!

Combine the powdered sugar and lemonade mix in a small bowl. Scoop the dough into balls about 2 tablespoons in size and roll between your hands until they're smooth. Roll the balls individually in the bowl of lemon powdered sugar, tossing them around the bowl until the balls are completely covered with sugar mix, then place them on the prepared baking sheets, 2 to 3 inches apart.

BAKE!

Bake the cookies at 350°F for 10 to 12 minutes, until golden brown around the edges. Using oven mitts, remove the baking sheets from the oven and cool the cookies completely on the baking sheets. Store in an airtight container for up to 1 week.

CINNAMON BUTTERSCOTCH COOKIES

Makes 18 to 24 cookies

You can tell a lot about a person by the type of cookie they like. There is nothing wrong with being a vanilla person—it's a classic, after all. Chocolate lovers tend to be a little wilder. The citrus crew likes to see the sunny side of life. But it's the cinnamon fans you need to watch out for. Their spice is always balanced with a bit of sweetness, which makes them unpredictable and warm and fuzzy all at the same time. I add butterscotch chips to the mix, making these a snuggly cousin to the classic chocolate chip cookie. Cinnamon fans, this one's for you!

FYI
The secret ingredient in these cookies is the milk powder; read up on it on page 19.

INGREDIENTS

1¾ cups flour

2 tablespoons nonfat milk powder

2 tablespoons ground cinnamon

1¼ teaspoons kosher salt

½ teaspoon baking powder

¼ teaspoon baking soda

2 sticks (16 tablespoons) unsalted butter, super soft

1¼ cups packed light brown sugar

1 egg

2 teaspoons vanilla extract

1 (11-ounce) bag butterscotch chips

EQUIPMENT

OVEN

2 BAKING SHEETS

BAKING SPRAY

MIXING BOWLS

MEASURING CUPS + SPOONS

WOODEN SPOON OR FIRM RUBBER SPATULA

FRIDGE (OPTIONAL)

ICE CREAM/COOKIE SCOOP

OVEN MITTS

PREP!

Preheat the oven to 350°F. Coat the baking sheets with baking spray.

MIX THE DRY!

In a medium bowl, mix the flour, milk powder, cinnamon, salt, baking powder, and baking soda.

MIX THE WET AND COMBINE!

In a large bowl, and using a wooden spoon or sturdy spatula, mix the butter and brown sugar, flexing your muscles for about 2 minutes, until they are fully combined. Add the egg and vanilla and stir until combined and fluffy, about 1 minute.

Add the dry mixture to the butter-sugar mixture, mixing until just combined. (If your dough is exceptionally wet—if it looks really shiny or oily—your butter was likely too hot. Throw it in the fridge for a few minutes to firm up before continuing on.)

BUTTERSCOTCH TIME!

Fold in the butterscotch chips.

SCOOP AND BAKE!

Scoop your dough into balls about 2 tablespoons in size and place them 2 to 3 inches apart on the prepared baking sheets. Bake at 350°F for 10 to 12 minutes, until the edges of the cookies are golden brown. With oven mitts, remove the baking sheets from the oven and cool the cookies completely on the baking sheets. Store in an airtight container for up to 1 week.

NOVEMBER

FYI
You want your butter to be soft and melty, not fully liquid and definitely not steaming hot. The best way to do this is in the microwave (in a microwave-safe bowl) on high for 30 seconds. If you need to heat it for longer (some microwaves are stronger than others), do it in 15-second bursts, and take a look at it between zaps.

FYI
If you like a smaller (or larger) cookie, go for it—you're the boss, after all! Keep in mind that a smaller scoop will bake faster (reduce the bake time by 2 to 4 minutes) and a larger scoop will bake longer (increase the bake time by 2 to 4 minutes).

POWER MUFFINS

Makes 12 muffins

Do you have a favorite shirt or pair of shoes, or a perfectly worn-in baseball hat that makes you feel like you can run faster, jump higher, knock the ball out of the park, or crush your turn in double Dutch? This muffin gives you the same unbeatable power. A few bites of this oaty, nutty, chocolaty number, and you will be ready to rake the yard into the biggest, most jump-in-able pile of leaves ever, or set the record for the most apples picked in an hour, or wherever else this perfect fall day takes you. It's my secret weapon every other season of the year, too.

FYI
If you don't have buttermilk, you can DIY your own by combining ½ cup milk with ½ tablespoon lemon juice or white vinegar, and letting it sit on the counter for 10 minutes. Use immediately!

INGREDIENTS

2 cups flour

2 teaspoons baking powder

½ teaspoon baking soda

½ teaspoon kosher salt

2 eggs

¾ cup sugar

½ cup buttermilk

1 teaspoon vanilla extract

1 cup vegetable oil

½ cup pure maple syrup

1 cup old-fashioned rolled oats

1 cup chopped pecans

½ cup chocolate chips

EQUIPMENT

OVEN

12-CUP CUPCAKE/MUFFIN PAN

12 PAPER CUPCAKE LINERS

MIXING BOWLS

MEASURING CUPS + SPOONS

WHISK

RUBBER SPATULA

TOOTHPICK

OVEN MITTS

PREP!

Preheat the oven to 375°F. Line the cups of the muffin pan with the cupcake liners.

MIX THE DRY!

In a large bowl, combine the flour, baking powder, baking soda, and salt.

WHISK THE WET AND COMBINE!

In a medium bowl, whisk together the eggs, sugar, buttermilk, and vanilla. Whisk in the oil and maple syrup. Add the wet ingredients to the dry ingredients and whisk until smooth. Stir in the oats, pecans, and chocolate chips.

FYI
The batter for these muffins is a tad wet because of the extra maple syrup!

SCOOP AND BAKE!

Using a measuring cup, spoon ⅓ cup of the batter into each cup of the muffin pan. The batter will reach right up under the lip of the liner (but shouldn't go over!). Bake the muffins at 375°F for 18 to 20 minutes, until the muffin tops brown slightly and a toothpick comes out clean when poked into the center of a muffin (see page 23). With oven mitts, take the pan out of the oven and let the muffins cool in the pan. These will last in an airtight container on your counter for 4 to 5 days.

NOVEMBER

MAC 'N' CHEESE PANCAKES

FYI
Leftover mac 'n' cheese works great for these!

Makes 8 pancakes

We all know and love the breakfast-for-dinner play, but why do we stop there? I vote that dinner can get in on the fun by making an appearance before noon. When I wake up with a savory craving and the morning lineup of sweets won't scratch my itch, I turn to my dinnertime BFF: mac 'n' cheese. Leftovers from the fridge are the hero of this cheesy, amazingly lumpy pancake, making it even easier to execute in the early morning hours.

INGREDIENTS

1 cup flour

2 tablespoons sugar

1 tablespoon + 1 teaspoon baking powder

1 teaspoon kosher salt

¾ cup milk

1 egg

3 tablespoons vegetable oil

2 cups cheesy mac 'n' cheese (any kind), cold or room temperature

FOR SERVING
Butter (optional)

WHISK THE DRY!

In a medium bowl, whisk together the flour, sugar, baking powder, and salt.

WHISK THE WET AND COMBINE!

In a small bowl, whisk together the milk, egg, and oil. Pour the wet mixture into the dry mixture and whisk until your pancake batter is mostly smooth. Stir in the mac 'n' cheese.

COOK!

Spray your nonstick pan or griddle with baking spray and warm it over medium heat. Pour ¼ cup of the batter onto the prepared pan or griddle. Cook until the batter has set on the bottom and browned (bubbles will begin to appear on the top and a few will burst), 1 to 2 minutes. Flip carefully with the spatula and cook the other side until golden brown, 1 to 2 minutes more. Remove the pancake to a plate and cover to keep warm. Spray the pan or griddle again and repeat to make the remaining pancakes, spraying before cooking each one. Serve warm with butter, if desired.

EQUIPMENT
MIXING BOWLS

MEASURING CUPS + SPOONS

WHISK

NONSTICK PAN OR GRIDDLE

BAKING SPRAY

PLASTIC SPATULA

NOVEMBER

S'MORES PANCAKE CAKE

Makes 1 large cake, serves 2 to 4

Everyone who has ever been camping knows the best thing about spending a night in the great outdoors: unlimited s'mores. Melty chocolate and toasted marshmallow, perfectly sandwiched between two pieces of graham cracker—it's guaranteed to leave your hands a sticky, brilliant mess. S'mores are the star of any camping trip I am on. And when I make these treats indoors, it feels more like being outdoors. I layer up this over-the-top campfire-inspired cake for a breakfast or a nighttime snack by the fireplace. Sticky hands optional.

FYI
If you are looking for a little edge in your breakfast game without s'mores-ing it up, this is a killer recipe for chocolate chip–graham pancakes.

INGREDIENTS

¾ cup flour

2 tablespoons light brown sugar

2 teaspoons baking powder

½ teaspoon kosher salt

½ cup milk

1 egg

1 tablespoon + 1 teaspoon vegetable oil

½ cup broken-up graham crackers

¼ cup chocolate chips

SERVING

½ cup Marshmallow Fluff

¼ cup chocolate syrup

EQUIPMENT

MIXING BOWLS

MEASURING CUPS + SPOONS

WHISK

NONSTICK PAN OR GRIDDLE

BAKING SPRAY

PLASTIC SPATULA

MIX THE DRY!

In a medium bowl, whisk together the flour, brown sugar, baking powder, and salt.

WHISK THE WET AND COMBINE!

In a small bowl, whisk together the milk, egg, and oil. Pour the wet mixture into the dry mixture and whisk until your pancake batter is mostly smooth. Stir in the graham cracker crumbs and chocolate chips.

COOK!

Spray the nonstick pan or griddle with baking spray and warm it over medium heat. Pour ¼ cup of the batter into

FYI
Substitute any type of marshmallow you have in place of the Marshmallow Fluff!

the prepared pan or onto the griddle. Cook until the pancake batter has set on the bottom and browned (bubbles will begin to appear on the top and a few will burst), 1 to 2 minutes. Flip carefully with the plastic spatula and cook the other side until golden brown, 1 to 2 minutes more. Remove the pancake to a plate and keep warm. Spray again with the baking spray and continue to make the pancakes, spraying before making each one.

SERVE!

Build your pancake layer cake. Place one pancake on the plate as your base, and spread half the marshmallow over it. Add the second pancake and spread the remaining marshmallow over it. Add the third pancake and pour the chocolate syrup over it all. Serve immediately.

BISCUIT EGGS IN A FRAME

Makes 6 square biscuits

When I have a crew of people staying over—you are never too old for a slumber party, FYI—my fave morning move is to set up Christina's Diner. I roll some knives and forks in napkins, fill up big mugs with coffee or cocoa, set up stools around my counter for guests, and write up a menu of options for breakfast. You can opt for Really Good Flapjacks (page 62) or Apple Pie Waffles (page 162) if that's your vibe, but these creamy eggs cooked *inside* a flaky, buttery biscuit are what Christina's Diner is really famous for—well, that and the friendly staff!

INGREDIENTS

3 cups flour, plus extra

1 tablespoon baking powder

1 teaspoon baking soda

1 teaspoon kosher salt

1½ sticks (12 tablespoons) unsalted butter, cold, cut into ¼-inch cubes (yes, that's tiny, but you can do it!)

1¼ cups heavy cream

SERVING

6 eggs

Kosher salt and pepper

EQUIPMENT

BAKING SHEET

BAKING SPRAY

MIXING BOWLS

MEASURING CUPS + SPOONS

BUTTER KNIFE

ROLLING PIN

RULER

PLASTIC SPATULA

FRIDGE

OVEN + OVEN MITTS

MICROWAVE-SAFE PLATE + MICROWAVE *OR* NONSTICK SKILLET + STOVETOP

PREP!

Coat the baking sheet with baking spray.

MIX THE DRY!

In a large bowl, combine the flour, baking powder, baking soda, and salt.

TOSS AND PINCH!

Add the butter to the dry ingredients and pinch with your fingers, working until you no longer see pieces of butter, about 2 minutes (see page 203). It should be a shaggy mix.

STREAM THE CREAM!

Add the cream, and mix gently with your hands to start. Once the cream is incorporated, start pressing and squeezing with your hands to bind the dough together.

ROLL AND CUT!

Dust a clean, dry section of your countertop with a little flour. Using a flour-dusted rolling pin, roll out your dough into a 6 by 9-inch rectangle that is about ½ inch thick (use a ruler!). Use a butter knife to cut the long side into 3 rows and the short side into 2 rows. You should have six 3-inch squares.

CHILL!

Transfer the biscuits to the prepared baking sheet and put them in the refrigerator to chill for 30 minutes. Meanwhile, preheat the oven to 425°F.

BAKE!

Bake at 425°F for 15 minutes, until the biscuits are golden brown at the edges. These are best served warm, but you can also stash them in an airtight container for up to 3 days.

(recipe continues)

PUT AN EGG IN IT!

Let your biscuits cool a bit, then use a butter knife to cut a 1½-inch hole in each biscuit. You'll know your hole is the perfect size if you can comfortably place an egg (in its shell) inside it!

BAKE THE EGGS!

Now that your holes are cut, you are ready to bake your eggs! You have two options:

Option 1: Microwave Method. Place a biscuit on a microwave-safe plate and crack an egg into the hole. Sprinkle a little salt and pepper on top and microwave for 1 minute and 30 seconds in 30-second intervals. Serve immediately.

Option 2: Stovetop Method. Preheat a nonstick skillet with a little butter on medium-low heat. Place the biscuit in the pan and crack an egg into the biscuit's hole. Sprinkle with a little salt and pepper and cook for 4 minutes. Using the plastic spatula, quickly flip the biscuit and cook for another 3 to 4 minutes. Serve immediately.

HAM AND JAM BISCUITS

Makes 6 square biscuits

*I do like
ham and jam.
I do like them, ma'am-I-am!*

*Would you like them in a
biscuit?
Would you like to try and
whisk it?*

*I do like them
every day.
I do like them
every way.
I do like them
near or far.
I do like them
where you are.*

*I do like
jam and ham.
I do like them,
Ma'am-I-am.*

NOVEMBER

INGREDIENTS

3 cups flour, plus extra for dusting

1 tablespoon baking powder

1 teaspoon baking soda

1 teaspoon kosher salt

1½ sticks (12 tablespoons) unsalted butter, cold, cut into ¼-inch cubes (yes, it's tiny, but you can do it!)

1¼ cups heavy cream

SERVING

12 thin ham slices

¾ cup jam, any flavor

EQUIPMENT

BAKING SHEET

BAKING SPRAY

MIXING BOWLS

MEASURING CUPS + SPOONS

BUTTER KNIFE

ROLLING PIN

RULER

PLASTIC SPATULA

FRIDGE

OVEN

OVEN MITTS

PREP!

Coat the baking sheet with baking spray.

MIX THE DRY!

In a large bowl, combine the flour, baking powder, baking soda, and salt.

TOSS AND PINCH!

Add the butter to the dry ingredients and pinch with your fingers, working until you no longer see pieces of butter, about 2 minutes. You should have a shaggy mix (see page 203).

STREAM THE CREAM!

Add the cream and mix gently with your hands to start. Once the cream is incorporated, start pressing and squeezing with your hands to bind the dough together.

ROLL AND CUT!

Dust a clean, dry section of your countertop with a little flour. Roll out the dough with a flour-dusted rolling pin to a 6 by 9-inch rectangle about ½ inch thick (use a ruler!). Use a butter knife to cut the long side into 3 rows and the short side into 2 rows, to make six 3-inch squares.

CHILL!

Place the biscuits on the prepared baking sheet and place in the refrigerator to chill for 30 minutes. Meanwhile, preheat the oven to 425°F.

BAKE!

Bake the biscuits at 425°F for 15 minutes, until they are golden brown at the edges. With oven mitts, remove them from the oven.

JAM IT UP!

When the biscuits have cooled slightly, use a butter knife to slice your biscuits in half lengthwise, then layer them each with 2 slices of ham and 2 tablespoons of jam—sandwich-style. Serve at once!

GRASSHOPPER CUPCAKES

Makes 12 frosted cupcakes

I have a lot of daydreams about what I want to be when I grow up. Some days I am a truck driver who gets to cruise across the country with my windows down and my music blasting. Other times I like to imagine I am an astronaut cartwheeling through space on the next mission to Mars. But my favorite possibility is that I own a little hotel in the mountains, complete with roaring fireplaces and new guests every day to befriend and feed. In my inn, there are fluffy quilts on the bed, cozy robes to cuddle up in, and a turn-down service that always comes with a chocolate mint cupcake to put on your pillow—I mean, you'd come for the cupcake alone, right?! Well, in case you beat me to my dream of running a hotel, I'll give you the recipe for those cupcakes.

1 batch (12) chocolate cupcakes (recipe follows)

1 batch (2 cups) mint chocolate frosting (recipe follows)

ASSEMBLE!

Dollop a large spoonful of chocolate frosting—about 2 tablespoons—on top of each cupcake. Use the back side of your spoon to smooth your frosting into an even and fluffy layer. Serve! Store in a large airtight container on the counter for up to 3 days or in the fridge for up to 1 week.

(recipe continues)

DECEMBER

CHOCOLATE CUPCAKES

Makes 12 cupcakes

INGREDIENTS

1¼ cups flour

½ cup cocoa powder

1 tablespoon baking powder

½ teaspoon kosher salt

½ stick (4 tablespoons) unsalted butter, melted

¾ cup sugar

3 tablespoons light brown sugar

2 eggs

½ cup vegetable oil

1½ teaspoons vanilla extract

½ cup buttermilk

PREP!

Preheat the oven to 350°F. Line the cups of the cupcake pan with the cupcake liners.

MIX THE DRY!

In a large bowl, combine your flour, cocoa powder, baking powder, and salt.

WHISK THE WET AND COMBINE!

In a medium bowl, whisk together your butter, sugars, and eggs until well combined. Whisk in the oil and vanilla. Whisk in the buttermilk. Then whisk the wet ingredients into the dry ingredients until smooth.

SCOOP AND BAKE!

Use a ¼-cup measure to scoop portions of your batter into the cups of the cupcake pan. The batter will be almost level with the top edge of the liner (but it shouldn't go over!). Bake at 350°F for 15 to 20 minutes, until the tops brown slightly and a toothpick poked into the center of a cupcake comes out clean (see page 23). Using oven mitts, remove the pan from the oven and let the cupcakes cool completely before removing from the pan.

FYI
If you don't have buttermilk, you can DIY your own by combining ½ cup milk with ½ tablespoon lemon juice or white vinegar, and letting it sit on the counter for 10 minutes. Use immediately!

EQUIPMENT

OVEN

12-CUP CUPCAKE/MUFFIN PAN

12 PAPER CUPCAKE LINERS

MIXING BOWLS

MEASURING CUPS + SPOONS

WHISK

RUBBER SPATULA

TOOTHPICK

OVEN MITTS

DECEMBER

MINT CHOCOLATE FROSTING

Makes 2 cups

INGREDIENTS

1½ sticks (12 tablespoons) unsalted butter, softened

2½ cups powdered sugar

6 tablespoons cocoa powder

2 tablespoons milk

¾ teaspoon mint extract

¼ teaspoon vanilla extract

¼ teaspoon kosher salt

MIX!

Starting on low speed, use the mixer to combine your butter, powdered sugar, and cocoa powder, 1 minute. Increase the mixer speed to medium and whip until super smooth, about 3 minutes. Turn off the mixer. Use your spatula to scrape down the sides of your bowl well.

ADD AND FLUFF!

Add the milk, mint and vanilla extracts, and salt. Continue mixing until combined and fluffy, about 1 minute.

EQUIPMENT

HAND MIXER OR STAND MIXER WITH
  PADDLE ATTACHMENT

MIXING BOWL

MEASURING CUPS + SPOONS

RUBBER SPATULA

DINNER SPOON

DEAR
Thanks.
The Pe

CINNAMON-BUN QUICK BREAD

Makes one loaf, 12 slices

Whether it's sending my mom a hilarious handmade card every year for her birthday or having cold pizza for New Year's Day breakfast, I am a big fan of traditions. To me there is nothing more fun and cozy than having a special thing that only you and the ones closest to you do together. No matter where I am on Christmas morning, I make this cinnamon-bun quick bread, frosted with cream cheese, for the family to eat as they tear open presents and pad around in their pajamas.

INGREDIENTS

CINNAMON SWIRL FILLING

1½ cups light brown sugar

¾ stick (6 tablespoons) unsalted butter, melted

2 tablespoons ground cinnamon

½ teaspoon kosher salt

THE DOUGH

2½ cups flour, plus more for dusting

⅓ cup sugar

2 teaspoons baking powder

½ teaspoon baking soda

½ teaspoon kosher salt

1 egg

¾ cup milk

½ stick (4 tablespoons) unsalted butter, melted

CREAM CHEESE FROSTING

1 (4-ounce) package cream cheese, room temperature

½ stick (4 tablespoons) unsalted butter, softened

1½ cups powdered sugar

½ teaspoon vanilla extract

⅛ teaspoon kosher salt

EQUIPMENT

OVEN

9 BY 5-INCH LOAF PAN

BAKING SPRAY

MIXING BOWLS

MEASURING CUPS + SPOONS

WHISK

WOODEN SPOON

CUTTING BOARD

ROLLING PIN

RULER

OVEN MITTS

BUTTER KNIFE

PREP!

Preheat the oven to 375°F and coat the loaf pan with baking spray.

MIX THE CINNAMON FILLING!

In a medium bowl, mix the brown sugar, butter, cinnamon, and salt.

MIX THE DOUGH!

In a large bowl, combine the flour, sugar, baking powder, baking soda, and salt. In a small bowl, whisk together the egg and milk, then with a wooden spoon, stir the eggy mixture into the dry ingredients until just combined. Stir in the melted butter. Finish off the mixing with your hands, pinching and squeezing to form your dough.

(recipe continues)

ROLL OUT, FILL, AND ROLL UP!

Sprinkle about a tablespoon of flour on your cutting board. Dust your rolling pin with a little flour as well. Roll out the dough into a 9 by 15-inch rectangle. Spread the cinnamon filling evenly over your dough, leaving a ½-inch border at each edge. Roll the dough up tightly, like you would roll up a sleeping bag, and place it in the prepared loaf pan, keeping the seam on the bottom.

BAKE!

Bake the loaf at 375°F for 50 to 55 minutes, until the top is a deep golden brown and the cinnamon goo bubbles up around the edges. Using oven mitts, remove the loaf pan from the oven and let the quick bread cool completely in the pan.

MIX THE FROSTING!

In a medium bowl, mix the cream cheese, butter, and sugar with a wooden spoon. Add the vanilla and salt and switch to stirring with a whisk. Cream cheese frosting is best when it's as fluffy and white as can be. This takes about 2 minutes of whisking intensely.

SLICE AND SERVE!

When the loaf is cool enough to handle (about 30 minutes after coming out of the oven), pop it out of its pan and place it on a serving plate. Frost your loaf with the cream cheese frosting, then slice and serve! Store in the refrigerator in an airtight container for up to 1 week.

GINGERBREAD CUT-OUT COOKIES

Makes 24 cookies, depending on size

Real talk: Do you like gingerbread? I know, I'm usually skeptical, too. In the wonderful world of holiday treats, gingerbread has about as bad a reputation as fruitcake. Usually dry and rarely delicious, it isn't at the top of anyone's holiday wish list. That's all about to change. These cookies have the spice and flair of gingerbread, but they are baked with a perfect ratio of flavor and snap. Leave 'em out for Santa as a last-minute bribe.

INGREDIENTS

2 cups flour, plus more for dusting

2 teaspoons ground ginger

1½ teaspoons cinnamon

½ teaspoon kosher salt

¼ teaspoon ground nutmeg

2 sticks (16 tablespoons) unsalted butter, softened

½ cup packed light brown sugar

2 tablespoons molasses

EQUIPMENT

2 BAKING SHEETS

BAKING SPRAY

MIXING BOWLS

MEASURING CUPS + SPOONS

WOODEN SPOON OR STAND MIXER WITH PADDLE ATTACHMENT

3 ZIP-TOP BAGS (OR PLASTIC WRAP)

FRIDGE

OVEN

ROLLING PIN

RULER

COOKIE CUTTERS

PLASTIC SPATULA

OVEN MITTS

PREP!

Coat the baking sheets with baking spray.

MIX THE DRY!

In a medium bowl, combine the flour, ginger, cinnamon, salt, and nutmeg.

MIX THE WET AND COMBINE!

In a large bowl, combine the softened butter, brown sugar, and molasses using a wooden spoon (or in a stand mixer). Mix until the butter and sugar are smooth, about 2 minutes by hand (or 45 seconds in a mixer). Add the dry ingredients to the butter mixture and stir or mix until smooth (if you're not using a mixer, it may be easiest to ditch the spoon and use your hands to form the dough).

SHAPE AND CHILL!

Form the dough into a ball, and divide the ball into 3 pieces. Place each piece into a plastic sandwich bag and pat the dough smooth and flat with your hands. Refrigerate the bags for 15 minutes. Meanwhile, preheat the oven to 350°F.

ROLL AND CUT!

Dust a clean, dry section of your countertop with a little flour. Take a piece of dough out of the plastic bag and place on the counter. Dust the rolling pin with a little flour and roll out the dough until it is ¼ inch thick (use a ruler!). Use your favorite cookie cutters to cut the dough into shapes. Using a spatula, lift the shapes and transfer them to the prepared baking sheets. Repeat with the remaining 2 packages of dough. If you use a range of cutter

(recipe continues)

DECEMBER

sizes and shapes, keep the bigger cut-outs on one baking sheet and the smaller cut-outs on the other baking sheet.

BAKE!

Bake the cookies at 350°F for 5 to 10 minutes (depending on the size of your cut-outs; 5 minutes for smaller, 10 minutes for larger cookies). Double-check that you have set the timer. Because these cookies are already dark brown, it's tricky to tell by sight when they're ready to take out of the oven. The timer is your best friend! With oven mitts, remove the baking sheets from the oven and cool the cookies completely on the baking sheets.

MAKE IT YOUR OWN!

Ready to get your Picasso on? Turn to page 144 to see our fave ways to decorate!

CANDY CANE LANE SHEET CAKE

Makes 24 slices

Like clockwork, I get a care package from my mom the first week of December every year. Yes, I am (kind of) a grown-up who still, proudly!, gets care packages from home. Filled with her normal newspaper clippings and family photos, the December package is *always* overflowing with more candy canes than I know what to do with. Here's my favorite use for these red-and-white treats: Smash those suckers and sprinkle them over a minty frosted sheet cake—perfect for holiday partying.

1 baked candy cane sheet cake (recipe follows)

1 batch (4 cups) peppermint frosting (recipe follows)

¼ cup crushed peppermint candy or candy canes

ASSEMBLE!

Place the sheet cake on an upside-down baking sheet or serving platter. Spread the peppermint frosting on the top of the sheet cake, using a rubber spatula and smoothing evenly to coat the whole surface. Top with bits of the crushed candy cane in whatever design you please! To serve, cut the cake into 4 lengthwise rows and 6 crosswise rows, for a total of 24 pieces. Wrap the leftover slices well in plastic and keep on the counter for up to 3 days or in the fridge for up to 1 week.

DECEMBER

(recipe continues)

CANDY CANE SHEET CAKE

Makes one 9 by 13-inch cake

INGREDIENTS

1¾ cups flour

1 tablespoon baking powder

½ teaspoon kosher salt

½ stick (4 tablespoons) unsalted butter, melted

¾ cup sugar

2 tablespoons light brown sugar

2 eggs

½ cup vegetable oil

2 teaspoons vanilla extract

½ cup buttermilk

¼ cup crushed peppermint candy or candy canes

PREP!

Preheat the oven to 350°F and coat the baking pan with baking spray.

MIX THE DRY!

In a large bowl, mix the flour, baking powder, and salt.

MIX THE WET AND COMBINE!

In a medium bowl, whisk together the butter, both sugars, and the eggs until well combined. Whisk in the oil and vanilla, then whisk in the buttermilk.

Whisk the wet ingredients into the dry ingredients until smooth.

SPRINKLE AND BAKE!

Pour the batter into the prepared baking pan and sprinkle the crushed candy cane pieces on top. Bake the cake at 350°F for 30 to 35 minutes, until it is golden brown and a toothpick comes out clean when poked into the center (see page 23). Using oven mitts, remove the cake pan from the oven and let it cool completely in the pan.

FYI
If you don't have buttermilk, you can DIY your own by combining ½ cup milk with ½ tablespoon lemon juice or white vinegar, and letting it sit on the counter for 10 minutes. Use immediately!

EQUIPMENT

OVEN

9 BY 13-INCH PAN

BAKING SPRAY

MIXING BOWLS

MEASURING CUPS + SPOONS

WHISK

ZIP-TOP PLASTIC BAG

ROLLING PIN

RUBBER SPATULA

TOOTHPICK

OVEN MITTS

BUTTER KNIFE

PEPPERMINT FROSTING

Makes 4 cups

INGREDIENTS

3 sticks (24 tablespoons) unsalted butter, softened

4½ cups powdered sugar

3 tablespoons milk

1 teaspoon mint extract

½ teaspoon kosher salt

½ cup crushed peppermint candy or candy canes

MIX!

Starting on low speed, use a mixer to combine the butter and sugar, 1 minute. Increase the mixer speed to medium and whip until super smooth, about 3 minutes. Turn off the mixer. Use your spatula to scrape down the sides of the bowl well.

ADD THE FLUFF!

Add the milk, mint extract, and salt and mix until combined and fluffy, about 1 minute. Add the candy canes and continue mixing for another 30 seconds.

EQUIPMENT

HAND MIXER OR STAND MIXER WITH
   PADDLE ATTACHMENT

MIXING BOWL

MEASURING CUPS + SPOONS

RUBBER SPATULA

COOKIES AND (ICE) CREAM SHAKES

Makes 2 shakes

Cookies on their own—pretty good, right? But an excuse to eat cookies *and* ice cream? At the same time? Slam dunk. Especially in winter when there are always holiday cookies on the counter. Though who are we kidding? This shake crushes year-round!

INGREDIENTS

4 large scoops of ice cream, your choice of flavor

½ cup milk

4 medium cookies, such as Oreos, or 2 large cookies

COMBINE AND BLEND!

Combine the ice cream, milk, and cookies in a blender, and blend for 45 seconds, or until you reach your preferred thickness.

DRINK UP!

Pour into glasses and have a blast. (Beware of brain freeze if you drink too quickly!)

FYI
Vanilla ice cream and Oreo cookies is the obvious classic combo, but this will work with any cookies, milk, and ice cream you have on hand. I'm a fan of holiday cut-out cookies and strawberry ice cream, or chocolate chip cookies and chocolate ice cream.

DECEMBER

EQUIPMENT

ICE CREAM/COOKIE SCOOP

MEASURING CUP

BLENDER

2 TALL GLASSES

birthday cookies,
page 224

chocolate birthday cookies,
page 225

BIRTHDAY COOKIES

Makes 18 to 24 cookies

I believe in delivering celebration in as many ways as possible. If you don't have time to get going with a layer cake or even a classic cupcake, these cookies deliver just as much excitement as a sprinkle-speckled birthday cake—I promise. And you don't even have to wait for a birthday. We have a chocolate version (see facing page), if that's more your speed. Just remember that birthday cookies need candles, too!

FYI
If you like a smaller (or larger) cookie, go for it—you're the boss, after all! Keep in mind that a smaller scoop will bake faster (reduce the bake time by 2 to 4 minutes) and a larger scoop will bake longer (increase the bake time by 2 to 4 minutes).

INGREDIENTS

2 cups flour

2 tablespoons nonfat milk powder

1¼ teaspoons kosher salt

½ teaspoon baking powder

¼ teaspoon baking soda

2 sticks (16 tablespoons) unsalted butter, super soft

¾ cup sugar

½ cup packed light brown sugar

1 egg

2 teaspoons vanilla extract

1 (12-ounce) bag white chocolate chips

¼ cup sprinkles, plus more for the top

FYI
The secret ingredient in these cookies is the milk powder; read up on it on page 19.

PREP!

Preheat the oven to 350°F. Coat the baking sheets with baking spray.

MIX THE DRY!

In a medium bowl, mix the flour, milk powder, salt, baking powder, and baking soda.

MIX THE WET AND COMBINE!

In a large bowl, and using a wooden spoon or sturdy spatula, mix the butter and both sugars, flexing your muscles for about 2 minutes, until they are fully combined. Add the egg and vanilla and stir until combined and fluffy, about 1 minute.

Add the dry mixture to the butter-sugar mixture, mixing until just combined. (If your dough is exceptionally wet—if it looks really shiny or oily—your butter was likely too hot. Throw it in the fridge for a few minutes to firm up before continuing on.)

SPRINKLES AND CHOCOLATE TIME!

Stir in the white chocolate chips and sprinkles.

SCOOP AND BAKE!

Scoop your dough into balls of about 2 tablespoons and place the balls 2 to 3 inches apart on the prepared baking sheets. Top the cookies with extra sprinkles. Bake the cookies at 350°F for 10 to 12 minutes, until the edges of the cookies are golden brown. With oven mitts, remove the baking sheets from the oven and cool the cookies completely on the baking sheets. Store in an airtight container for up to 1 week.

EQUIPMENT

OVEN

2 BAKING SHEETS

BAKING SPRAY

MIXING BOWLS

MEASURING CUPS + SPOONS

WOODEN SPOON OR FIRM RUBBER SPATULA

MICROWAVE + MICROWAVE-SAFE BOWL (OPTIONAL)

FRIDGE (OPTIONAL)

ICE CREAM/COOKIE SCOOP

OVEN MITTS

CHOCOLATE BIRTHDAY COOKIES

Makes 18 to 24 cookies

It probably goes without saying, but these cookies are for the chocolate lover in your life.

FYI
You want your butter to be soft and melty, not fully liquid and definitely not steaming hot. The best way to do this is in the microwave (in a microwave-safe bowl) on high for 30 seconds. If you need to heat it for longer (some microwaves are stronger than others), do it in 15-second bursts, and take a look at it between zaps.

INGREDIENTS

1⅔ cups flour

¼ cup cocoa powder

2 tablespoons nonfat milk powder

1¼ teaspoons kosher salt

½ teaspoon baking powder

¼ teaspoon baking soda

2 sticks (16 tablespoons) unsalted butter, super soft

¾ cup sugar

½ cup packed light brown sugar

1 egg

2 teaspoons vanilla extract

1 (12-ounce) bag chocolate chips

¼ cup sprinkles, plus more for the top

EQUIPMENT

2 BAKING SHEETS

BAKING SPRAY

MIXING BOWLS

MEASURING CUPS + SPOONS

WOODEN SPOON OR FIRM RUBBER
    SPATULA

MICROWAVE + MICROWAVE-SAFE
    BOWL (OPTIONAL)

OVEN

FRIDGE (OPTIONAL)

ICE CREAM/COOKIE SCOOP

OVEN MITTS

PREP!

Preheat the oven to 350°F. Coat the baking sheets with baking spray.

MIX THE DRY!

In a medium bowl, mix the flour, cocoa powder, milk powder, salt, baking powder, and baking soda.

MIX THE WET AND COMBINE!

In a large bowl, and using a wooden spoon or sturdy spatula, mix the butter and both sugars, flexing your muscles for about 2 minutes, until they are fully combined. Add the egg and vanilla and stir until combined and fluffy, about 1 minute.

Add the dry mixture to the butter-sugar mixture, mixing until just combined. (If your dough is exceptionally wet—if it looks really shiny or oily—your butter was likely too hot. Throw it in the fridge for a few minutes to firm up before continuing on.)

CHOCOLATE TIME!

Stir in the chocolate chips and sprinkles.

SCOOP AND BAKE!

Scoop your dough into balls of about 2 tablespoons and place the balls 2 to 3 inches apart onto the prepared baking sheets. Top the balls with extra sprinkles. Bake the cookies at 350°F for 10 to 12 minutes. Double-check that you set the timer. Because these cookies are already dark brown, it's tricky to tell by sight when they're ready to take out of the oven. With oven mitts, remove the baking sheets from the oven and cool the cookies completely on the baking sheets. (Store in an airtight container for up to 1 week.)

B-DAY CEREAL SQUARES

Makes 15 squares

Whether the birthday you are celebrating is your mom's or your pet rock's, these b-day cereal squares take the party up a notch. With vanilla for that extra level of flavor and sprinkles because everyone knows it is not a celebration without sprinkles, even Sylvester the Stone will be begging for seconds.

FYI
The marshmallows will balloon up in a hilarious way when you microwave them, so make sure you use an oversize bowl.

INGREDIENTS

½ cup sprinkles

5 tablespoons unsalted butter (save the paper it's wrapped in!)

1 (10.5-ounce) bag marshmallows

2 teaspoons vanilla extract

7 cups Rice Krispies cereal

FYI
Swap the cereal for whatever you love most (or whatever you've got in the cupboard)!

PREP!

Coat the baking pan with baking spray. Fully cover the bottom of the prepared pan with the sprinkles.

MELT!

In a very large microwave-safe bowl, melt the butter and marshmallows together in the microwave for 2 minutes. Remove from the microwave and stir, then microwave for 1 more minute. Stir until smooth. Stir the vanilla extract into the melted marshmallows.

CEREAL TIME!

Add the Rice Krispies to the marshmallow mixture and stir with a spatula until every bit is coated.

SPREAD AND COOL!

Scrape the mixture into the baking pan and spread evenly with a greased spatula or with the butter paper (my grandma taught me this!). Let cool until firm, 15 to 20 minutes, then cut into 3 lengthwise rows and 5 crosswise rows to make a total of 15 treats. Store in an airtight container on your counter for up to 5 days.

EQUIPMENT

9 BY 13-INCH BAKING PAN

BAKING SPRAY

MICROWAVE + LARGE MICROWAVE-
   SAFE BOWL

RUBBER SPATULA

MEASURING CUPS + SPOONS

B'DAY SHORTCAKE SUNDAES

Makes 9 mini sundaes

One of my absolute, all-time, hands-down favorite creations is ice cream cake. I mean, the combination of the smooth ice cream and cold, pillowy cake gets me every time. While I love this frozen innovation, I don't always have the time—or patience, if I am being honest—to freeze and unfreeze, and wrestle ice cream into a cake shape. I need my ice cream cake combo on demand, and this b-day shortcake sundae is my go-to solution.

INGREDIENTS

1¾ cups flour

½ cup sugar

⅓ cup packed light brown sugar

2 teaspoons baking powder

2 teaspoons kosher salt

1 egg

¼ cup heavy cream

2 teaspoons vanilla extract

1½ sticks (12 tablespoons) unsalted butter, cold, cut into ¼-inch cubes (yes, that's tiny, but you can do it!)

½ cup sprinkles

1 cup powdered sugar

SERVING

Ice creams, flavors of choice

EQUIPMENT

OVEN

BAKING SHEET

BAKING SPRAY

MIXING BOWLS

MEASURING CUPS + SPOONS

WHISK

BUTTER KNIFE

WOODEN SPOON

ICE CREAM/COOKIE SCOOP OR
    LARGE SPOON

OVEN MITTS

PREP!

Preheat the oven to 350°F and coat the baking sheet with baking spray.

MIX THE DRY!

In a large bowl, mix the flour, both sugars, the baking powder, and salt.

CRACK AND WHISK!

Crack the egg into a small bowl and whisk it thoroughly with the cream and vanilla.

TOSS AND PINCH!

Add the butter to the dry ingredients and pinch with your fingers, working until you no longer see pieces of butter, about 2 minutes. You should have a shaggy mixture.

STREAM THE CREAM!

Add the cream mixture and stir gently with a wooden spoon until incorporated, about 30 seconds. Mix in the sprinkles. Let the dough rest for 5 minutes in the bowl.

SCOOP AND ROLL!

Scoop out the dough into balls of about 3 tablespoons each.

Pour the powdered sugar into a small bowl and roll each dough ball in the sugar to coat well. Transfer the dough balls to the prepared baking sheet, placing them 2 inches apart.

BAKE!

Bake at 350°F for 13 minutes, until golden brown at the edges. Using oven mitts, take the baking sheet out of the oven and let the shortcakes cool briefly.

SERVE!

Serve warm or at room temperature with a scoop or two of your favorite ice creams—we like to go for a variety of colors and flavors. These are best served right away, but you can also stash them in an airtight container for up to 3 days.

BIRTHDAY PANCAKES

Makes 6 to 8 pancakes

In my family, we like to celebrate birthdays from sunrise to sunset. You better believe that, as soon as your eyes pop open on your special day, we will be showering you with love and attention. One way we squeeze extra b-day into the day is with a special sprinkle-filled, vanilla-y morning meal. Candles and singing (at the top of your lungs, in your best operatic impression) are optional but highly encouraged.

INGREDIENTS

1 cup flour

2 tablespoons sugar

1 tablespoon + 1 teaspoon baking powder

½ teaspoon kosher salt

½ cup milk

1 egg

3 tablespoons vanilla extract

3 tablespoons vegetable oil

¾ cup white chocolate chips

⅓ cup sprinkles

SERVING

1 batch (½ cup) vanilla glaze (recipe follows)

WHISK THE DRY!

In a medium bowl, whisk together the flour, sugar, baking powder, and salt.

WHISK THE WET AND COMBINE!

In a small bowl, whisk together the milk, egg, vanilla, and oil. Pour the wet mixture into the dry mixture and whisk until the pancake batter is mostly smooth. Stir in the white chocolate chips.

COOK!

Coat the nonstick pan or griddle with baking spray and warm it over medium heat. Place 1 teaspoon of the sprinkles in the prepared pan or on the griddle, then pour ¼ cup of the batter over the sprinkles. Top the batter with another 1 teaspoon of the sprinkles. Cook until the pancake batter has set on the bottom and browned (bubbles will begin to appear on the top and a few will burst), 1 to 2 minutes. Flip carefully with a plastic spatula and cook the other side until golden brown, 1 to 2 minutes more. Remove the pancake and place on a plate. Spray the pan or griddle again and continue to make the pancakes. Spray each time before adding the sprinkles and batter.

SERVE!

Drizzle as much or as little of the glaze over the pancakes and dig in while still warm!

VANILLA GLAZE

EQUIPMENT

MIXING BOWLS

MEASURING CUPS + SPOONS

WHISK

NONSTICK PAN OR GRIDDLE

BAKING SPRAY

PLASTIC SPATULA

Makes ½ cup

INGREDIENTS

½ cup powdered sugar

1 tablespoon vanilla extract

WHISK!

In a bowl, whisk together the powdered sugar and vanilla until well combined and smooth.

SHOUT-OUTS

To Shannon Salzano, Jena Derman, and Alex Watkins—my bodyguards, my most creative counterparts, my sisters in cookbooking: Thank you for always being down to take on the craziest of projects, for not blinking an eye when it's time to eat our weight in Corn Dog Waffles or the illustrious Dreamsicle Blondies (more Tang!). I'm pretty sure the expression "ride or die" was invented because of you three.

To Henry Hargreaves (feat. Blue): Thank you to the most brilliant photographer and wrangler of puppies, children, and food, for taking such gorgeously spirited shots.

To Kim Witherspoon: Put your cape away already, Wonder Woman! You're giving all of us wannabes a complex with your insane ability to serve and protect. :)

To the coolest publishing house around, Clarkson Potter: Thank you, Aaron Wehner, for pushing us to bring our inner kids out to play. Francis Lam, your willingness to cannonball into our crazy ideas and make them better never ceases to amaze me. Marysarah Quinn, for making us look good. Every. Single. Time.

To our biggest inspiration—KIDS! Iris and Charlotte are not only excellent nieces but also headstrong gals who gave their honest opinion and cutest poses at the drop of a hat. Amalia, Zahir and Zahara, Charlotte (Purple!), Roshi, Grover and Caleb, Ian and Delilah, you are STARS! Just remember where you got your first break, okay? And thanks for bringing your parents along, too, I guess.

To my fierce women who keep me forever humble—Grandma, Mom, and Sissy: You brought me up in the kitchen, you celebrate me, you push me. You taught me the meaning of baking, you cleaned up my messes, and, finally, you let me eat as much cookie dough as I pleased.

To my Milk Bar family: There is no better example of undercover grown-ups than you. Your ideas and spirit in and out of the kitchen keep me inspired every day to bring more lightness, nostalgia, and joy to this crazy world.

To my husband, Will: Thank you for the adventure that is life—for celebrating my epic overall collection, for buying me matching scooters because no other present would do, for never throwing shade when there are six batches of cookies in the freezer, for reminding me there's no such thing as too many hot dogs (especially in the Corn Dog Waffle), and for letting us turn our home upside down coworking while writing/baking for this book. Home is where you (and Butter) are.

To the people who brought the cool stuff in these photos: Thank you, Rachel Blumenthal and Rockets of Awesome, for the insanely fun wardrobe; Sierra Tishgart and Great Jones, because every human deserves a brilliant blue baking sheet; and Larry Witt and OXO, for all the best kitchen tools.

INDEX

Note: Page references in *italics* indicate photographs.

A

Apple(s)
  -a-Day Cereal Squares, 188, *189*
  Gooey Cinnamon, 164, *164*
  Pie Waffles, 162–65, *163*

B

Bacon-Cheddar Cornbake
    Muffins, 128, *129*
Baking powder, 17
Baking soda, 17
Baking spray, 17
Banana(s)
  Chunky Monkey Smoothies, *75, 77*
  Crunch Bread, *56, 57–58*
  Monkey in the Middle
    Muffins, 74, *76*
  ripeness stages, 58–59
Bars. *See also* Cereal Squares
  Dreamsicle Blondies, 82
  Easy as Pie, 84, *85*
  Gazillionaire's, *96, 97*
  Triple Layer Cheesecake, 30, *31*
  White Chocolate Blondies, *52, 53*
Bird Bread, 66, *67*
Birthday
  Cereal Squares, *226, 227*
  Cookies, 222, *224*
  Cookies, Chocolate, *223, 225*
  Pancakes, *230, 231*
Biscuit(s)
  Cheddar Chive, *72, 73*
  Eggs in a Frame, 200, 201–2

Ham and Jam, 204, *205*
Blondies
  Dreamsicle, 82
  White Chocolate, *52, 53*
Blueberry(ies)
  All-the-Fruit Smoothies, *120, 121*
  Berries and Cream Muffins, *122, 123*
  -Lemon Pancakes, 78, *79*
Bread(s)
  Banana Crunch, *56, 57–58*
  Bird, 66, *67*
  Cinnamon-Bun Quick, *210, 211–12*
  Cornbread, 118, *119*
  French Toast Muffins, 28, *29*
  Pizza, 176, *179*
Breakfast
  Apple Pie Waffles, 162, *163*
  Bacon-Cheddar Cornbake
    Muffins, 128, *129*
  Berries and Cream Muffins, *122, 123*
  Birthday Pancakes, *230, 231*
  Biscuit Eggs in a Frame, 200, 201–202, *203*
  Blueberry-Lemon Pancakes, 78, *79*
  Cheddar Chive Biscuits, *72, 73*
  Chocolate Muffins, 112, *113*
  Compost Pancakes, 38, *39*
  French Toast Muffins, 28, *29*
  Ham and Jam Biscuits, 204, *205*
  Jack-o'-Lantern Muffins, 184, *185*
  Leftover Waffle, 86, *87*
  Mac 'n' Cheese Pancakes, 196, *197*

Monkey in the Middle
    Muffins, 74, *76*
  Power Muffins, *194, 195*
  Really Good Flapjacks, 62, *63*
  Rise and Shine Cereal
    Squares, *70, 71*
  Tropical Mermaid Muffins, *106, 107*
  Veggie Frittata Bites, 80, 81
Butter, 17
  Grape, 118, *119*
  Honey, 99, *99*
  Peanut Butter–, 58
Buttermilk, 18
Butterscotch
  Cinnamon Cookies, 192, *193*
  Compost Cereal Squares, 150, *152*
  Compost Pancakes, 38, *39*

C

Cakes
  Candy Cane Lane Sheet, *216, 217–19*
  Candy Cane Sheet, 218
  Chocolate, Thin, 149
  S'mores Pancake, *198, 199*
  Tea, Raspberry-Lemon
    Ricotta, 98–99, *99*
Candy, in Trick-or-Treat
    Quakes, *186, 187*
Candy Cane(s)
  Lane Sheet Cake, *216, 217–19*
  Peppermint Frosting, 219
  Sheet Cake, 218
Cereals, 18. *See also* Cereal
    Squares
  Choco Crunch Cookies, 48, *49*

Cereals (*continued*)
  Chunky Monkey Smoothies, *75, 77*
  Gazillionaire's Bars, *96, 97*
  Pot o' Gold Shakes, *60, 61*
  Snap Crackle Pop Shakes, *116, 117*
Cereal Squares
  Apple-a-Day, 188, *189*
  B-Day, 226, 227
  Cherry Pie, 150, 151
  Citrus Surprise, *64, 65*
  Coco Cabana, *32, 33*
  Compost, 150, 152
  PB&J, *166, 167*
  Rise and Shine, 70, 71
  Rocky Road, *54, 55*
Cheese. *See also* Cream cheese
  Bacon-Cheddar Cornbake Muffins, 128, 129
  Cheddar Chive Biscuits, *72, 73*
  Mac 'n', Pancakes, *196, 197*
  Pizza Bread, 176, *179*
  Raspberry-Lemon Ricotta Tea Cake, 98–99, *99*
  Veggie Frittata Bites, *80, 81*
Cheesecake Bars, Triple Layer, 30, *31*
Cherry Pie Cereal Squares, 150, 151
Chocolate, 18. *See also* White Chocolate
  Birthday Cookies, 223, 225
  Black and White Cupcakes, 168–71, *169*
  Building Blocks Cookie Sandwiches, 34, *35–37*
  Cake, Thin, 149
  Cake Waffles, German, *46, 47*
  Chip Cookies, Best Ever (to Me, Anyway), *134, 135*
  Choco Crunch Cookies, 48, *49*
  Coconut Cupcakes, 92, *93–95*

Compost Cereal Squares, 150, 152
Compost Pancakes, 38, *39*
Cupcakes, 170, 208
Cut-Out Cookies, 26, 27, 36
DIY Ice Cream Sandwiches, 146–49, *147*
Frosting, Dark, 37, 95, *95*
Gazillionaire's Bars, *96, 97*
Grasshopper Cupcakes, 206–9, *207*
Mint Cookies and Cream Cookie Pie, 88, 89–90, *91*
Mint Frosting, 209
Monkey in the Middle Muffins, 74, *76*
Muffins, 112, *113*
Power Muffins, *194, 195*
Rocky Road Cereal Squares, *54, 55*
S'mores Pancake Cake, *198*, 199
Snap Crackle Pop Shakes, *116, 117*
Triple Layer Cheesecake Bars, 30, *31*
Cinnamon
  Apples, Gooey, *164, 164*
  -Bun Quick Bread, 210, *211–12*
  Butterscotch Cookies, 192, *193*
  Cupcakes, 182
  Sugar and Peach Shortcakes, *136, 137–39*
Cocoa powder, 18
Coconut, 18
  Berry Loco Cupcakes, 40, *41–43*
  Chocolate Cupcakes, 92, *93–95*
  Coco Cabana Cereal Squares, *32, 33*
  Cupcakes, 42, 94
  German Chocolate Cake Waffles, *46, 47*

Granola Cookies, 100, 101
Tropical Mermaid Muffins, *106, 107*
Compost Cereal Squares, 150, 152
Compost Pancakes, 38, *39*
Cookies. *See also* Bars
  adding to baked goods, 18
  Birthday, 222, 224
  Birthday, Chocolate, 223, 225
  Choco Crunch, 48, *49*
  Chocolate Chip, Best Ever (to Me, Anyway), *134, 135*
  Chocolate Cut-Out, 26, 27, 36
  Cinnamon Butterscotch, 192, *193*
  and Cream Cookie Pie, Mint, 88, 89–90, *91*
  and (Ice) Cream Shakes, 220, *221*
  crumbles, added to shakes, 18
  Cut-Out, 141–43, *144–45*, 156
  Cut-Out Sandies, 103
  Earth Day, 68, 69
  Gingerbread Cut-Out, 213–14, *215*
  Granola, 100, 101
  Lemonade Zing, 190, *191*
  Nut-n-Jammie Cookie Sammies, 102, *102–3*
  Nutty Sandies, 172, *173*
  preparing, tips for, 50
Cookie Sandwiches
  Building Blocks, 34, *35–37*
  Fluffernutter, 154, *155–56*
Cornbake Muffins, Bacon-Cheddar, 128, 129
Cornbread, 118, *119*
Corn Dog Waffles, 124, 125
Cornmeal, 18
  Cornbread, 118, *119*
  Corn Dog Waffles, 124, 125
Cream, heavy, 18

Cream cheese
  Cinnamon-Bun Quick Bread, 210, 211–12
  Triple Layer Cheesecake Bars, 30, 31
Cupcakes
  Berry Loco, 40, 41–43
  Black and White, 168–71, 169
  Chocolate, 170, 208
  Chocolate Coconut, 92, 93–95
  Cinnamon, 182
  Coconut, 42, 94
  Grasshopper, 206–9, 207
  Pumpkin Patch, 180, 181–83
  Strawberries and Cream, 108, 109–11
  Vanilla, 110

D

Dog Biscuits (Give a Dog a Biscuit), 174, 175
Donut Shakes, 114, 115
Dreamsicle Blondies, 82
Drink mixes, for recipes, 18

E

Eggs, 18
  in a Frame, Biscuit, 200, 201–2
  Veggie Frittata Bites, 80, 81
Extracts, 18

F

Floats, Purple Cow, 126, 127
Flour, 18
Fluffernutter Cookie Sandwiches, 154, 155–56
French Toast Muffins, 28, 29
Frostings
  Dark Chocolate, 37, 95, 95
  Dreamy Vanilla, 171
  Mint Chocolate, 209
  Peppermint, 219
  Pumpkin, 183

Raspberry, 43
Strawberry, 111
Fruit, 18. *See also specific fruits*
  All-the-, Smoothies, 120, 121

G

German Chocolate Cake Waffles, 46, 47
Gingerbread Cut-Out Cookies, 213–14, 215
Glazes
  Lemon, 78
  Vanilla, 231
Graham crackers
  Compost Pancakes, 38, 39
  S'mores Pancake Cake, 198, 199
  Triple Layer Cheesecake Bars, 30, 31
Granola Cookies, 100, 101
Grape(s)
  Butter, 118, 119
  Flower Power Smoothies, 160, 161
Grape soda
  Purple Cow Floats, 126, 127

H

Ham and Jam Biscuits, 204, 205
Honey Butter, 99, 99
Hot dogs. See Corn Dog Waffles

I

Ice Cream
  Anything Goes Shakes, 158, 159
  B'Day Shortcake Sundaes, 228, 229
  Cookies and (Ice) Cream Shakes, 220, 221
  Donut Shakes, 114, 115
  Popcorn Shakes, 177, 178
  Pot o' Gold Shakes, 60, 61
  Purple Cow Floats, 126, 127

Sandwiches, DIY, 146–49, 147
Snap Crackle Pop Shakes, 116, 117
Snow, 44, 45
Trick-or-Treat Quakes, 186, 187

J

Jams & jellies
  Easy as Pie Bars, 84, 85
  Grape Butter, 118, 119
  Ham and Jam Biscuits, 204, 205
  Nut-n-Jammie Cookie Sammies, 102, 102–3
  PB&J Cereal Squares, 166, 167

K

Kitchen rules, 14–15
Kitchen tools, 20–21

L

Lemonade Zing Cookies, 190, 191
Lemon Glaze, 78

M

Mac 'n' Cheese Pancakes, 196, 197
Marshmallow Fluff, 19
  Dreamsicle Blondies, 82
  Fluffernutter Cookie Sandwiches, 154, 155–56
  S'mores Pancake Cake, 198, 199
Marshmallows, 19
  Apple-a-Day Cereal Squares, 188, 189
  B-Day Cereal Squares, 226, 227
  Cherry Pie Cereal Squares, 150, 151
  Choco Crunch Cookies, 48, 49

Marshmallows (*continued*)
 Citrus Surprise Cereal
  Squares, 64, 65
 Coco Cabana Cereal Squares,
  32, 33
 Compost Cereal Squares, 150,
  152
 PB&J Cereal Squares, 166, 167
 Rise and Shine Cereal
  Squares, 70, 71
 Rocky Road Cereal Squares,
  54, 55
 Snap Crackle Pop Shakes,
  116, 117
Measuring ingredients, 22
Milk, for recipes, 19
Mint. *See also* Peppermint
 Chocolate Frosting, 209
 Cookies and Cream Cookie
  Pie, 88, 89–90, 91
Muffins
 Bacon-Cheddar Cornbake,
  128, 129
 Berries and Cream, 122, 123
 Chocolate, 112, 113
 French Toast, 28, 29
 Jack-o'-Lantern, 184, 185
 Monkey in the Middle, 74, 76
 Power, 194, 195
 Tropical Mermaid, 106, 107
 Veggie Frittata Bites, 80, 81

N

Nonfat milk powder, 19
Nut butters, 19. *See also* Peanut
  Butter
 Rocky Road Cereal Squares,
  54, 55
Nut(s), 19
 Citrus Surprise Cereal
  Squares, 64, 65
 Cut-Out Sandies, 103

-n-Jammie Cookie Sammies,
  102, 102–3
 Nutty Sandies, 172, 173
 Power Muffins, 194, 195
 Rocky Road Cereal Squares,
  54, 55

O

Oats, 19
 Banana Crunch Bread, 56,
  57–58
 Bird Bread, 66, 67
 Compost Cereal Squares, 150,
  152
 Compost Pancakes, 38, 39
 Power Muffins, 194, 195
Oil, 19
Orange(s)
 Flower Power Smoothies,
  160, 161
 Peaches and Cream
  Smoothies, 120, 121

P

Pancakes
 Birthday, 230, 231
 Blueberry-Lemon, 78, 79
 Cake, S'mores, 198, 199
 Compost, 38, 39
 Mac 'n' Cheese, 196, 197
 Really Good Flapjacks, 62, 63
Pantry ingredients, 17–19
Peach(es)
 and Cinnamon Sugar
  Shortcakes, 136, 137–39
 and Cream Smoothies, 120,
  121
 Gooey, 138, 139
Peanut Butter
 –Butter, 58
 Fluffernutter Cookie
  Sandwiches, 154, 155–56

Monkey in the Middle
  Muffins, 74, 76
 PB&J Cereal Squares, 166,
  167
 Triple Layer Cheesecake Bars,
  30, 31
Pepitas, Toasted, 184
Peppermint
 Candy Cane Lane Sheet Cake,
  216, 217–19
 Candy Cane Sheet Cake,
  218
 Frosting, 219
Pizza Bread, 176, 179
Popcorn Shakes, 177, 178
Potato chips
 Compost Cereal Squares, 150,
  152
Pretzels, 19
 Compost Cereal Squares, 150,
  152
 Compost Pancakes, 38, 39
 Gazillionaire's Bars, 96, 97
Pumpkin
 Frosting, 183
 Give a Dog a Biscuit, 174,
  175
 Jack-o'-Lantern Muffins, 184,
  185
 Patch Cupcakes, 180, 181–83

Q

Quakes, Trick-or-Treat, 186,
  187

R

Raspberry(ies)
 All-the-Fruit Smoothies, 120,
  121
 Berry Loco Cupcakes, 40,
  41–43
 Frosting, 43

-Lemon Ricotta Tea Cake,
98–99, *99*
Rules of the kitchen, 14–15

S
Salt, 19
Seeds
    Bird Bread, 66, *67*
Shakes
    Anything Goes, 158, *159*
    Cookies and (Ice) Cream, 220,
        221
    Donut, 114, *115*
    Popcorn, 177, *178*
    Pot o' Gold, *60, 61*
    Snap Crackle Pop, *116,* 117
    Trick-or-Treat Quakes, *186,* 187
Shortcake(s)
    Cinnamon Sugar and Peach,
        136, 137–39
    Strawberry, 130–33, *131*
    Sundaes, B'Day, 228, *229*
Smoothies
    All-the-Fruit, 120, 121
    Chunky Monkey, 75, *77*
    Flower Power, *160,* 161
    Peaches and Cream, 120, 121
    Watermelon Lime, 104, *105*
S'mores Pancake Cake, *198,* 199
Snow Ice Cream, *44, 45*
Sour Cream, Whipped, 132, 165
Sprinkles
    B-Day Cereal Squares, 226, 227
    B'Day Shortcake Sundaes, 228,
        229
    Birthday Cookies, 222, 224
    Birthday Pancakes, *230,* 231
    Building Blocks Cookie
        Sandwiches, 34, 35–37
    Chocolate Birthday Cookies,
        223, 225

Strawberry(ies)
    All-the-Fruit Smoothies, *120,*
        121
    and Cream Cupcakes, *108,*
        109–11
    Frosting, 111
    Macerated, *133, 133*
    Shortcakes, 130–33, *131*
Sugar, 19
Sundaes, B'Day Shortcake, 228,
    229

T
Tools of the trade, 20–21
Toothpick test for doneness, 23
Trick-or-Treat Quakes, *186,* 187
Troubleshooting, 24–25

V
Vanilla
    Cupcakes, 110
    Frosting, Dreamy, 171
    Glaze, 231
    Whipped Cream, *139, 139*
Veggie Frittata Bites, 80, 81

W
Waffles
    Apple Pie, 162–65, *163*
    Corn Dog, 124, 125
    German Chocolate Cake, 46,
        47
    Leftover, 86, *87*
Watermelon Lime Smoothies,
    104, *105*
Whipped Cream, Vanilla, 139, *139*
Whipped Sour Cream, 132, 165
White Chocolate
    Berries and Cream Muffins,
        122, 123
    Birthday Cookies, 222, 224
    Birthday Pancakes, 230, 231

Blondies, *52, 53*
Dreamsicle Blondies, 82
Mint Cookies and Cream
    Cookie Pie, 88, 89–90, *91*

Y
Yogurt
    Chunky Monkey Smoothies,
        75, *77*
    Peaches and Cream Smoothies,
        120, 121

PRODUCTION CREDITS:
Photographer: **Henry Hargreaves**
Photography Assistant:
    Blue Monte Hamel
Production Assistant:
    Alexandra Watkins
Creative Director: **Shannon Salzano**
Recipe Developer & Food Stylist:
    Jena Derman

Designer: **Marysarah Quinn**
Production Manager: **Derek Gullino**
Editor: **Francis Lam**
Production Editor: **Patricia Shaw**
Composition: **Merri Ann Morrell** and
    Hannah Hunt
Indexer: **Elizabeth Parson**